LOOKING BACK AT BRITAIN

DECADENCE AND CHANGE

1920s

LOOKING BACK AT BRITAIN

DECADENCE AND CHANGE

1920s

Jonathan Bastable

Reader's Digest | gettyimages

CONTENTS

1920s IMAGE GALLERY

FRONT COVER: High above the traffic on the streets of the City of London, two men work on the demolition of a partially collapsed building in 1927. With no safety equipment, they unpick the walls brick by brick from the top down.

BACK COVER: A little girl in a hand-knitted dress gazes into the mouthpiece of a tuba as the instrument's owner takes a break during the National Brass Band Festival at Crystal Palace in 1923.

TITLE PAGE: Fashionable guests at Ascot in June 1925.

OPPOSITE: The Pearly King and Queen of Finsbury pose with their pearly children in a donkey cart in 1925.

FOLLOWING PAGES:

Construction workers take their lunchbreak perched high up a half-finished building in April 1929.

Crowds gather near Giggleswick, North Yorkshire, to view the total eclipse of the Sun in June 1927. Such an eclipse had not been seen in Britain since 1724; the next would not occur until 1999.

The Debenham sisters pose on their BSA motorcycles on 23 September, 1925.

A group of boys caught skinny-dipping in the Serpentine in London's Hyde Park are chased off by one of Britain's first serving policewomen.

FIT FOR HEROES

Britain at the dawn of the Twenties was a nation lost in grief and confusion. Barely a year had passed since the Armistice had brought the Great War to an end and the after-echoes of the guns still hung in the air. Bereavement was an almost universal reality. Everybody had lost a friend or a brother, a father or a son in the war. Each family's sorrow was a private affair, but Britain as a whole had yet to grasp the cataclysm that had overtaken it. Life could not return to something resembling normality until the country came to terms with its monstrous loss.

SOLEMN OCCASION The coffin of the unknown soldier is escorted to Westminster Abbey by Field Marshal Douglas Haig, who had commanded the British Expeditionary Force during the war. In the Twenties, Haig devoted himself to the welfare of ex-servicemen.

A DAY OF REMEMBRANCE

The British people had a need to mourn as never before and out of their longing grew an idea for a monument, a collective headstone, for the nation's many dead. That yearning found a focus when the architect Edwin Lutyens was commissioned to build a temporary structure on Whitehall as part of the victory parade held to mark the completion of the Versailles Treaty. His Cenotaph or 'empty tomb' was designed and built of wood and plaster in just two weeks. On Peace Day – 19 July, 1919 – the serried ranks of Allied troops marched past and gave it the salute, and through that act of homage Lutyen's piece of stage scenery unexpectedly took on a well-nigh magical significance. 'Near the memorial there were moments of silence when the dead seemed very near', wrote the correspondent of the *Morning Post*, 'when one almost heard the passage of countless wings. Were not the fallen gathering in their hosts to receive their comrades' salute and take their share in the triumph they had died to win?'

In the days that followed, people came in their thousands to the Cenotaph and placed wreaths upon it, as if it were a place of burial. The austere design of the memorial was quickly acknowledged as a perfect expression of the national feeling. 'Simple, grave and beautiful', said *The Times*, 'it has been universally recognised as a just and fitting memorial of those who have made the greatest sacrifice. And the flowers which have daily been laid upon it since the march show the strength of its appeal to the imagination.'

A permanent memorial

By the end of the month the government had decreed that a permanent stone Cenotaph, a replica of the wood-and-plaster original, should be built and unveiled on the second anniversary of the Armistice: 11 November, 1920. As the plans for the day were being laid another proposal emerged, the brainchild of an army chaplain named David Railton who had served on the front line. Railton wrote of how he had first conceived the idea one evening in 1916, at the height of the war: 'I came back from the line at dusk. We had just laid to rest the mortal remains of a comrade. I went to a billet near Armentières. At the back of the billet was a small garden, and in the garden a grave. At the head of the grave there stood a rough cross of white wood. On the cross was written in deep black-pencilled letters, "An Unknown British Soldier" ... I remember how still it was. Even the guns seemed to be resting. How that grave caused me to think. Later on I wrote to Sir Douglas Haig to ask if the body of an "unknown" comrade might be sent home.'

Railton received no reply, but the thought stayed with him. In August 1920 he sent a version of his proposal to Bishop Ryle, the Dean of Westminster, who passed the letter on to the King and the Prime Minister, David Lloyd George. The King thought the suggestion rather distasteful, a somewhat superfluous addition to the unveiling of the new Cenotaph, but Lloyd George saw the genius in it: here was a chance to create a rite that would have national and personal significance for all British citizens and perhaps go some way to healing the wounds of war.

In October the proposal to re-inter one anonymous soldier in Westminster Abbey was approved and the process of selecting his remains was set in motion.

GUARD OF HONOUR
The body of the unknown soldier at the Channel port of Boulogne in France, with a combined guard of honour drawn from both British and French forces. Marshal Ferdinand Foch, generalissimo of the French army and (from March 1918) supreme commander of the Allied armies, came to the quayside to pay his last respects. He can be seen, standing with head bowed, just behind the two French soldiers at the rear of the carriage. Following a brief ceremony, the coffin was carried on board the HMS *Verdun* for the short sea voyage to England.

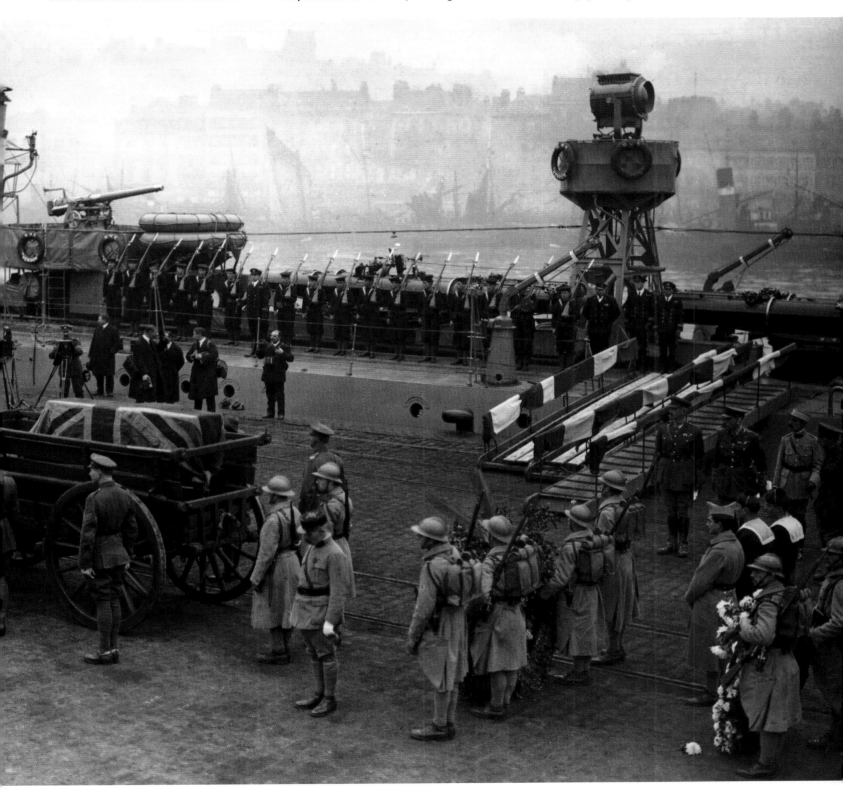

'[The Cenotaph] is so noble a thing … the war has moved you and lifted you above yourself.'

J M Barrie, in a letter to Edwin Lutyens

On 7 November, 1920, four work parties in France were sent out into the main British battlefields of the war – the Aisne, Somme, Arras and Ypres. Each party exhumed a body, which was examined to make sure that it was unidentifiable but definitely British. The four bodies were laid in plain deal coffins and placed in the chapel at St Pol.

At the stroke of midnight, Brigadier General L J Wyatt, then commander of British forces in France, entered the chapel and laid a hand on one of the four coffins. That coffin was sent on to Boulogne, where it was placed inside a beautifully crafted sarcophagus, made from an oak that had grown in the park of Hampton Court Palace. The oak casket was sealed with heavy iron bands, which also held in place a crusader sword from the personal collection of George V, who was now warming to the idea. The body of the unknown soldier was carried back to Britain on a destroyer, where it was met with a 19-gun salute from the

THE EMPTY TOMB
The giant Union Jacks fall away from the Cenotaph in the moment of unveiling on the second national Remembrance Day, Sunday 11 November, 1920. The word cenotaph comes from the Greek meaning 'empty tomb'. When the body of the deceased was lost, the ancient Greeks would sometimes perform a symbolic funeral and bury an empty sarcophagus. After the Great War, when so many thousands of men had died and been lost without trace, the form of the cenotaph seemed singularly appropriate. Lutyens' monument was much praised for the classic simplicity of its design, though some critics thought its symbolism was inappropriately unchristian.

battlements of Dover Castle. On 10 November the coffin was conveyed by train to London, and all along the way people thronged the stations, standing in silence, heads bared, waiting to pay their respects as the funeral train passed by.

The next day, Sunday 11 November, 1920, two solemn ceremonies took place. Early in the morning, at Victoria Station, the coffin of the unknown soldier was set on a gun carriage harnessed to six black horses, and draped in a Union Jack that had been carried through the war and was literally 'dyed with the blood of British soldiers'. An ordinary soldier's tin helmet was placed on top and the coffin then began its long procession through the huge crowds towards Westminster Abbey. 'The Unknown Warrior, in his daydreams in France, may have pictured his homecoming to himself, fancying how England would look on the day he came back to it', mused the correspondent of *The Times*. 'He never could have imagined a more lovely English day than was the day of his homecoming. It was a perfect late autumn day in London, with a touch of frost in the air, a veiled blue sky, and sun that would soon break through in full splendour.'

The procession took nearly two hours to reach Whitehall, where it was met by King George. As Big Ben struck the eleventh hour, the King pressed a button and the flags that covered the Cenotaph fell away to reveal the monument 'clean and wonderful in its naked beauty. Big Ben ceased, and the very pulse of Time stood still. In silence, broken only by a nearby sob, the great multitude bowed its head.

MOUNTAIN OF FLOWERS
The unveiling of the permanent Cenotaph on Sunday 11 November, 1920, was followed by a mass pilgrimage of mourners. All that day, throughout the night and the whole of the next day, the queue to file past never disappeared. It was at its shortest in the small hours of Monday morning, but by midday the line of people stretched all the way up Whitehall to Trafalgar Square and back again. By Monday evening, the monument was almost buried beneath the thousands of fading bouquets.

LEST WE FORGET

Memorials to the war dead sprung up all over Britain in the course of the Twenties. Some of the most poignant and impressive memorials were not on British soil, but were erected across the Channel in Flanders, where half a generation of British youth had met its death. One such monument is the Menin Gate (top), on the outskirts of the town of Ypres in Belgium. The names of Commonwealth soldiers who were lost and have no grave were to be carved on the walls of its vast Hall of Memory, but on completion it was found that there was not nearly enough space for them all. Although 55 thousand men are commemorated here, the names of another 34 thousand were inscribed on the Tyne Cot memorial near Passchendaele.

War memorials in Britain tended to be local, and so were on a smaller scale. Some, like the main memorial in the London borough of Southwark (centre), took the form of statuary: a determined Tommy wading through the mud, or a grim-faced sentry in a cape, his head bowed in sorrow. The most modest forms of war memorial were also the most common: a Celtic cross in a churchyard, as in the Bodmin Police Memorial (bottom), a plaque in a railway station or town hall, or a simple obelisk on a village green. And always a sad list of names, perhaps accompanied by a biblical verse: 'Their name liveth for evermore'.

Over all the Empire and the world's seas, men's hands had dropped from their toil and voices were hushed, and cities and peoples stood frozen.'

The King fell in behind the coffin, which proceeded the short distance to the Abbey. A thousand war widows waited inside, along with a hundred recipients of the Victoria Cross. There were no foreign dignitaries in the congregation. The coffin was borne to a grave at the west end of the nave and lowered gently into the ground. The King scattered some French soil on top, and the pit was later filled with earth – 100 sandbags' full – brought from the battlefields of Flanders. The ceremony was over by noon, but for the rest of the day and for many days after people queued for hours to file down Whitehall to Lutyen's empty tomb, then on to the fresh grave in the Abbey. The stream of mourners still flowed in the middle of the next week, by which time the Cenotaph was practically obscured by the many thousands of wreaths and bouquets.

> ## 'It can be said of each one: "He is not missing; he is here."'
> **Field Marshal Lord Plumer, at the unveiling of the Menin Gate, 1927**

SHORT BOOM, LONG SLUMP

That Remembrance Day in 1920 was perhaps the last moment of true national unity in what was to be a decade of political turmoil and industrial strife. In the election campaign of 1918, Lloyd George had said: 'We have just emerged from a great peril. And now what is our task? To make Britain a fit country for heroes to live in. Don't let us waste this victory merely in ringing joybells.' He intended his remark as a call to arms for a time of peace, a statement of the challenge that lay ahead. But what people grabbed hold of was the undertaking – slightly misremembered then and ever since – to create a 'land fit for heroes'.

For a time it seemed that the government was keeping its word. For two years after the war, the country enjoyed an economic boom. Factories of all sorts had been kept busy for years by government contracts, and had turned a good profit for their owners. Now that the fighting was over, industry switched to producing consumer goods for the masses. Many families had seen their incomes swell to twice the size or more during the years that the womenfolk were engaged in paid work for the war effort and the men's pay packets – earned in the trenches – piled up at home. Some soldiers came back with gratuities of up to £40, at a time when the average weekly wage was about £2. The time had come to spend, and the shops were piled high with things to buy.

But the boom was short-lived, an illusion that brought no lasting good. It would take more than a post-war spending spree to turn the the country into a land for returning heroes. For one thing, the main beneficiaries of the cash-rich years were not the returning officers and enlisted men, but the people who had never gone away. For the veterans of Flanders, Lloyd George's words had seemed

WITHIN THESE WALLS
As late as 1926 this mother and her five children were living in a cell in Worcester's disused prison. They were among the many victims of the chronic shortage of homes. The loss of many skilled builders during the war, combined with the slow demobilisation of those who did survive, contributed to a housing crisis after the war. Yet local authorities had an obligation to house the destitute – hence the strange and somewhat demeaning turn of events that led to this family and others going to a jail with an unlocked door.

to promise two things: a place to live and a job to earn a living by. As it turned out, neither was forthcoming. Viscount Walter Long, First Lord of the Admiralty until 1919, had said of the demobbed men: '… to let them come back from the horrible waterlogged trenches to something little better than a pigsty here would be criminal, a negation of all that has been said'. But in the year up to March 1920 only 715 new homes were built in England and Wales, even though the government estimated that 600,000 were required. Some ex-soldiers camped out in abandoned railway carriages or hastily constructed canvas huts – barely larger than a shed and no warmer or drier than a tent. There were instances, literally echoing the words of Viscount Long, in which ex-soldiers did end up making their homes in disused pig-sheds.

'A man who is frankly seeking a job is
not a welcome guest.'

Ex-battery commander writing in February 1920

LOOKING FOR A LIVING

Returning servicemen, young and old, often found that they were all but unemployable. Some accepted work as street peddlers (left), taking a role at the very bottom of the retail hierarchy. Old soldiers often wore their campaign medals on their coats, hoping that sympathy from the public might elicit more sales. It was little short of begging. Matches were one of the most widely sold commodities – everyone needed matches to light the stove or their cigarettes.

Former army officers often found themselves in financial straits almost as dire as those faced by the working-class soldiers who had served under them. These two officers (below), both with families to support, were making a political point wearing masks of shame as they operated a hurdy-gurdy on Whitehall. Some ex-officers made a living by hiring themselves out as dancing partners at swish London venues. And it was said in jest that you could not get a job as a West End chorus boy unless you were the holder of the Military Cross.

The search for work

The crisis in housing was matched by an equally acute and disappointing shortage of jobs. The disillusion over employment prospects was eloquently expressed by one ex-battery commander, writing in February 1920: 'During the War, all those who put on the King's uniform had a great access of friends. We were heroes in those days … When at last we came home, were demobilised and doffed our uniforms, we realised how much our welcome had depended on the glamour of our clothes, with all that they implied. In mufti we were no longer heroes, we were simply "unemployed" … I know there is no "right to work" in the economic sense, but the community owes a debt which it can and ought to pay … Are you going to withhold payment until it is too late?' It became too late at the end of 1920 – about the time that the first crop of cut flowers on the Cenotaph was wilting and dying. The dismay of many ex-soldiers turned to anger as unemployment began to rise. The jobless count passed a million in 1921, never again to dip below that point at any time during the decade.

Men in paid work were in a barely less precarious position than their workless fellows. As the economy returned to its peacetime rhythms, employers in the heavy industries – the coalmines in particular – assumed they could reimpose the Victorian conditions that had existed before the war. The mine-owners wanted to go back to the system where wages varied from one mine to another, depending on the changeable overhead costs of extracting the coal. The unions saw this as an attempt to divide and rule, and they were determined to resist. In the spring of 1921, a 'Triple Alliance' of miners, railwaymen and transport workers downed

tools. A general strike loomed, and the government declared a state of emergency. Political rallies turned into pitched battles between striking workers and massed ranks of police. Armed soldiers were posted on the streets of many big cities. The nationwide stoppage did not materialise, but nonetheless a staggering 89 million working days were lost to industrial action in the course of the year.

Time for a British revolution?

In their comfortable suburban homes, shopkeepers and bank managers worried that a revolution was brewing, that a hard core of British Bolsheviks were waiting for their moment to stage a coup, just as their Russian comrades had done four years before. There was certainly enough rumour and circumstantial evidence of a 'Red Peril' to frighten the jittery bourgeoisie. For example, when Remembrance Day came round again on 11 November, 1921, one wreath laid at the monument bore the bitter inscription 'To the dead victims of Capitalism, from the living victims of Capitalism' – it was deemed offensive and removed by police. One

WORKERS OF THE WORLD
The British Communist Party was founded in 1920. One of its most effective agitators was Wal Hannington, seen addressing a crowd of the unemployed in Trafalgar Square in 1922 (above). Though still in his early twenties, Hannington was a leading light in the National Unemployed Workers' Movement, which organised many of the hunger marches that took place in the early Twenties. He was arrested in 1925 under the 1797 Incitement to Mutiny Act, and sentenced to a year's imprisonment.

END OF THE ROAD

David Lloyd George was described by the economist John Maynard Keynes as 'this extraordinary figure of our time, this siren, this goat-footed bard, this half-human visitor to our age from the hag-ridden magic and enchanted woods of Celtic antiquity'. This strangely overwrought description seems merely to be a hostile way of saying that Lloyd George was a charismatic Welshman in a position of authority over Englishmen. Winston Churchill, who knew Lloyd George well, said more generously that he was 'the greatest master of getting things done and putting things through that I ever knew'. But that practical talent for achieving results had deserted Lloyd George by the end of his premiership. As a statesman, he failed to persuade the great nations to sort out the international chaos left at the end of the war. As Prime Minister, he could not mitigate the effects of the economic crisis that engulfed the country. By the time this photograph of him was taken, in September 1923, he had been out of power for almost a year.

CHILDREN OF THE MINES
The life of a child in the mining villages
of the north was always tough, made
tougher in times of strikes and disasters.
Children as young as this girl in Wigan –
photographed during the miners' strike of
1921 – were often expected not only to look
after younger brothers and sisters, but also
to bring lunch to the pithead. In the
evenings they were often turfed out onto
the street so that their fathers had the
space and privacy to fill a tub and wash off
the grime of the pit.

IDLE HANDS
Striking miners in Wigan take the children to hear a little backstreet oratory. In March 1921 Britain's mine owners decided they could no longer sustain the relatively high wages that had been paid during the war. Unilaterally, they cut miners' wages and locked the gates to any workers who did not agree to the new terms. The miners' union called its members out on strike, fully expecting the dockers and railway workers to come out in sympathy. But not for the last time the miners were left to go it alone.

decorated soldier marched down Whitehall wearing not his medals, but the tickets he had got when he was forced to pawn them. Close to the Cenotaph, members of the newly minted British Communist Party distributed newspapers to individuals in the unhappy crowds.

The year 1922 saw the first of the hunger marches that would later become such a feature of the 1930s. But the spectacle of long columns of men marching on London could easily be interpreted as a threat to law and order. The marchers were desperate, hungry men asking for help; but with their grim, pinched faces and red banners they looked worryingly like the belligerent vanguard of the proletariat, flexing its revolutionary muscle. It certainly appeared that way to Prime Minister Lloyd George, who remarked darkly that his government 'could not take risks

WORK AND PLAY
'Hopping' was an annual holiday for poor urban children, and also a chance for their mothers to do some paid work. As many as a quarter of a million people migrated to Kent at the end of August for the hop-picking season. About a third of them came from the East End of London. Families were generally accommodated in communal huts made of corrugated iron. But the regiments of hoppers spent much of their leisure time as well as their working hours in the open air – resting, eating food cooked on an open fire and giving the children a scrub with a soapy wet flannel.

with labour. If we did, we should at once create an enemy within our own borders, and one which would be better provided with dangerous weapons than Germany.'

In the end it was not the workers who brought down the government, but the Conservative members of Lloyd George's parliamentary coalition. The Tories had never liked or trusted the 'Welsh wizard' – he was a Liberal, after all – but they had allied themselves to him at a time when his claim to be 'the man who won the war' still rang true. Four years on, he was looking like the man who had lost the peace. In the summer of 1922, it became known that Lloyd George had amassed huge political funds by selling honours to anyone who could afford them: knighthoods could be had for £12,000, baronetcies for £30,000. In October the parliamentary Conservative party voted to cut their links with the Prime Minister. It was the end of the line for Lloyd George – and also for the Liberal party, which has not headed a government in Britain since.

THE HIGH TIDE OF EMPIRE

The politics of Empire were in a state of flux. The war had changed the balance of power in the wider world, and at the beginning of the decade it appeared that Britain and her Empire had benefited. Certainly, Britain emerged from the war with no rivals for world supremacy among the former powers of Europe. The Austro-Hungarian Empire had fallen apart and in its place there had arisen a jigsaw of independent nations with exotic and barely pronounceable names, such as Czechoslovakia and Yugoslavia. The Ottoman Empire had melted away like a snowfall in spring, and here too a new nation was taking shape: the secular republic of Turkey. Russia, under its new Bolshevist rulers, was at war with itself and out of the geopolitical game for the time being.

Germany was laid low. Her imperial assets in Africa had been added to Britain's formidable portfolio, giving the British Empire in the immediate post-war years a greater geographical extent than ever before. This fact alone was proof, if any were needed, that Britons were the world's pre-eminent nationality. To ensure that the upcoming generation shared in that assurance, every classroom in the land was decorated with a map on which the places ruled by Britain were coloured red. But schoolroom maps did not show how fragile and uncertain was Britain's hold on some of those overseas territories.

> ‘Without the Empire we should be tossed like a cork in the cross-current of world politics. It is at once our sword and our shield.’
>
> **William Morris Hughes, British-born prime minister of Australia, speaking in 1926**

There was not, as yet, any strong movement for independence in dominions such as Australia, Canada and New Zealand, although even there the horrific cost of the war in terms of young men's lives led some to question the ultimate authority of the ‘Mother Country’. But elsewhere, independence movements were gathering momentum. And nowhere was the demand for freedom more insistent than in Ireland, the most volatile corner of the whole empire.

Ireland on the brink of war

Ireland had been part of the United Kingdom since 1801, with elected Irish MPs sitting in the Westminster Parliament. But then, in the general election of December 1918, Sinn Fein swept to victory with 73 of Ireland's 105 seats and instead of becoming MPs in London they set up their own Irish parliament in Dublin – the Dáil. The day that the Dáil met for the first time, on 21 January, 1919, Irish ‘volunteers’ killed two members of the Royal Irish Constabulary (RIC) in Tipperary. The shots that killed those two policemen were the opening salvo in the Irish War of Independence (also known as the Anglo-Irish War) that lasted for more than two years. They were also the beginning of a guerilla strategy in which Irish police and British soldiers – 43,000 troops were stationed in Ireland – were targeted as ‘agents of a foreign power’.

continued on page 34

THE ARCHITECTS OF IRISH INDEPENDENCE

Among the most talented advocates of Irish independence was Arthur Griffith (above left), who had founded the Sinn Fein political party in 1905. Griffith was a theorist as well as an activist; he argued that the union of the British and Irish crowns in 1801 was illegal and that Ireland still constituted a separate monarchy. He suggested that Ireland might become an autonomous state under the British monarch, but this idea was unpalatable to out-and-out republicans. Michael Collins, the 'big fellow' (above right), was a brilliant military commander who master-minded the guerrilla war against the British in Ireland. Both men took part in the Anglo-Irish Treaty talks in London, having been appointed to the delegation by Eamon

de Valera, seen here (right) in dark hat and overcoat, taking the salute of an IRA division in County Clare in 1921. De Valera was president of Sinn Fein throughout the Anglo-Irish War, but spent most of the time in the USA raising funds. Astutely, he avoided taking part in the talks in London and so, unlike Griffith and Collins, was not tainted by signing the Anglo-Irish Treaty in July 1921. De Valera went on to found Fianna Fail (Warriors of Destiny); under his leadership the party ruled Ireland from 1932 to 1948. Neither Griffith nor Collins survived the fateful year of 1922. Griffith died of a haemorrhage, aged 50, on 12 August, 1922. Ten days later, Collins was shot dead by his former colleagues when his car was ambushed near Bandon in County Cork.

'Early this morning, I signed my death warrant.'

Michael Collins, speaking to his friend John O'Kane
after signing the Anglo-Irish Treaty on 6 December, 1921

WAR ZONE
On December 11, 1920, Cork city centre was burned to the ground (below). Cork was a focus of resistance to the British presence in Ireland, and the burning of the city was the culmination of reprisals there by the Black and Tans. The immediate catalyst was an IRA ambush in which a British soldier was killed. That night, fires broke out in and around Patrick Street. The superintendent of Cork fire brigade saw 'forty or fifty men walking in a body in the centre of Patrick Street, coming towards us in very mixed dress – some with khaki coats, some with khaki trousers, and some wore glengarry caps'. Among the buildings burned that night were the City Hall (with all the municipal records) and the Carnegie Library. At first, the authorities denied that British soldiers were involved – then later blamed the arson on renegade auxiliaries.

The Black and Tans

Prime Minister Lloyd George responded to the terrorist tactics adopted by the Irish volunteers by declaring Sinn Fein illegal and having the party's leaders arrested. This action was swiftly followed by a recruitment campaign in mainland Britain to bolster the ranks of the demoralised RIC. Seven thousand men signed up, many of them ex-soldiers grateful to have the chance of some paid work. There were not enough green RIC uniforms for the new recruits, so they were kitted out in military khaki and black belts, giving rise to the name by which they became notorious – the Black and Tans.

The methods of the Black and Tans were brutal and attracted growing criticism not just in Ireland but also in mainland Britain. The main tactic was to answer every attack on the forces of law and order with a bloody reprisal. They kicked in doors, sacked villages, burned the centre of Cork to the ground – then shot at Irish firemen trying to douse the flames. They viciously maltreated anyone suspected of being a 'shinner' and terrorised the civilian population on the assumption (broadly true) that practically everyone in southern Ireland was a Sinn Fein sympathiser. On a particularly infamous occasion – Bloody Sunday,

BLOODY SUNDAY

Covert operations were a feature of the Anglo-Irish war. Both sides used spies and infiltrators to gather intelligence. The Cairo Gang (right) was a group of British agents working in Dublin in 1920. Their mission was to prepare a 'hit list' of republicans and IRA members – in effect, a list of candidates for assassination – to the British military authorities. But the IRA's Intelligence Department had an informant in the Dublin police force who gave the IRA the names and addresses of the entire Cairo Gang. On Sunday 21 November, 1920, in a coordinated operation planned by Michael Collins, IRA men burst into the hotels and guesthouses where individual members of the gang were boarding. Some of the British spies died fighting; most were summarily executed on the spot. One of the gang, Lieutenant Donald Maclean, asked not to be shot in front of his wife; his attackers granted his request and took him up to the roof to kill him there. In all, 14 British agents were shot that morning, but the bloodshed had only begun. Later that same day – one of several 'Bloody Sundays' in Irish history – detachments of Black and Tans burst into a gaelic football match taking place in Croke Park, Dublin, supposedly on the trail of some of the gunmen. They opened fire on spectators and players, killing 14 unarmed Irish civilians, including the captain of one of the teams; six more people were wounded. The final act of Bloody Sunday came that evening, when three IRA prisoners held at Dublin Castle were 'shot trying to escape'.

PRAYING FOR PEACE

Both in Ireland and in mainland Britain, there were many people who were appalled by the uncontrolled and escalating violence. In 1921, while treaty negotiations were underway in London, a group of Irish Catholics (right) gathered at the wooden gates of Downing Street – erected in 1920 as a protection against terrorist attack – and recited a rosary for peace in Ireland. Their prayers went unanswered.

A DISUNITED REPUBLIC

The Anglo-Irish Treaty, signed in 1921, caused a split in Sinn Fein and in its armed wing, the IRA. Most of those in the higher ranks of the IRA were in favour of the treaty, and agreed with Michael Collins' tactical assessment that the IRA was not strong enough to continue the fight against the British. But the rank-and-file was split. A majority of Irish volunteers objected to the treaty because it did not bring total independence for all of Ireland, and because they believed that they could defeat the British army on Irish soil. As fighting broke out between the two factions in the summer of 1922, anti-treaty IRA men like these (left) showed their strength by parading with their weapons down Grafton Street in Dublin.

After the declaration of the Irish Free State in 1922, the British government washed its hands of southern Ireland. The Black and Tans were withdrawn and disbanded. But many Irish republicans were not satisfied with the terms of the treaty between Britain and the Free State. In particular, they objected to the symbolic oath of allegiance to the King that Irish parliamentarians were expected to make. Fighting broke out and escalated between pro-treaty republicans, who had taken over power from the British, and anti-treaty hardliners. The Anglo-Irish War of Independence segued into an Irish Civil War that cost the lives of many hundreds of Irishmen. In Dublin, Michael Collins was forced to order his troops (right, foreground) to shell the anti-treaty Republican army, which had established its headquarters in the Four Courts (the domed building in the background).

21 November, 1920 – they opened fire on the players and spectators at an ongoing gaelic football game in Croke Park, Dublin, killing 14 people including the captain of the Tipperary team, Michael Hogan.

The separation of Ireland

Inevitably, the outrages of the Black and Tans stoked the fires of hatred. Droves of young Irishmen rushed to join the ranks of the Irish volunteers, now increasingly known as the Irish Republican Army (IRA). The change of name made sense, because the Irish were now fighting the British in an all-out war of independence.

Yet even as the shootings and ambushes were going on, the Government of Ireland Act was making its way through Parliament in Westminster. The act made provision for six counties of Ulster to remain an integral part of the UK, in line with the wishes of their largely Protestant population, but proposed that the rest of the country become an 'Irish Free State' with dominion status like, say, Canada and Australia. The two Irelands came into being in 1922. It was not the end of the violence, but at least most of Ireland was now on its way to full independence.

Agitation in India – and massacre at Amritsar

Irish independence was a shocking event for many English people, who considered Ireland an unalienable part of Britain, but even more unthinkable was the idea that India should ever be anything but a British colonial possession. Yet far away on the subcontinent an independence movement was gathering momentum.

As in Ireland, the post-war chapter began in blood and violence. In April 1919 three Europeans were killed in Amritsar during anti-British rioting. A lady missionary was dragged off her bicycle and beaten by the mob. Three days later, a large and entirely peaceful crowd of Indians gathered in a walled garden near the centre of the city. They were ordered to disperse by the local British commander, General Reginald Dyer, but they remained seated on the ground. So the general ordered his troops – Gurkhas and Sikh auxiliaries – to fire into the crowd and to keep firing 'until their ammunition was exhausted'. Nearly 400 people were killed and more than a thousand wounded. In the days that followed, the unrepentant Dyer ordered that all Indians on the street where the English lady had been attacked should crawl its entire length on their bellies.

The news of the Amritsar massacre unleashed a fresh wave of agitation for independence. During this upswell of anti-British feeling a new leader emerged. He was an Indian lawyer, recently returned from South Africa, and his name was Mohandas Gandhi. He was steeped in the ancient philosophies of his native land, and he had also been deeply influenced by his reading of the Sermon on the Mount. His thinking had brought him to the conclusion that non-violent resistance

INSPECTING INDIA'S WOUNDED
During a visit to Bombay in 1921, Edward the Prince of Wales meets Indian troops who had been wounded and maimed while fighting for Britain in the First World War. India still furnished loyal soldiers to the British crown, but Britain's hold on India was beginning to slip as nationalism took hold beyond privileged intellectual circles. Jawaharlal Nehru, writing of the annual meeting of the Congress party in 1921, said it changed from being 'an English-knowing upper-class affair into a mass movement'. It was at this convention that a tricolour of saffron, white and green was adopted as India's national flag – though almost 30 more years were to pass before India emerged as a true independent nation.

to British rule was the only moral way to win independence, and so he formulated a strategy that he called *satyagraha* – the force of truth. It involved Indians boycotting British goods (everyone was encouraged to weave cloth for their own clothes), refusing to use British services such as the bus network and declining to work in British institutions such as law courts, schools and the armed forces.

Not everyone understood or agreed with Gandhi's peaceful, revolutionary idea. The political turmoil in India saw frequent outbreaks of violence between the Hindu majority and the Muslim minority. In 1922 insurgent Hindu peasants attacked a police station and killed 22 officers inside. Gandhi was held to be somehow responsible and imprisoned by the British. He was released two years later, and carried on the campaign to get the British to go home.

Squeezing Germany

From the perspective of the Twenties, the uprisings inside the Empire looked like unpleasant aftershocks of the war. But at least the main aim of the war – the subjection of Germany – seemed to have been achieved. To the great satisfaction of the mass of British people, the German state was disarmed and German cities were occupied by the troops of the victorious nations. What is more, Germany was being made to pay for her militarism in cold hard cash. Under the terms of the Versailles Treaty, the German state was to reimburse the Allies for all 'loss and damage' incurred by the war; the total monetary value was later set at 269 billion gold marks. Quite how Germany was supposed to find the money was not clear. Lloyd George spoke vaguely of making Germany 'turn out her pockets'; Sir Eric Geddes, Controller of the Navy, expressed it more graphically: 'We will squeeze Germany like a lemon. We will squeeze her until you can hear the pips squeak.'

In the event, the harsh treatment of Germany by the victors in the war produced squeaking noises of a very different nature – that of highly polished jackboots. In Bavaria, paramilitary organisations grew strong on the resentment that ordinary Germans felt against the perceived unfairness of the Versailles Treaty. In May 1923 *The Times* correspondent in Munich reported wryly on the activities of one of these organisations, the Bavarian National Socialist Workers party. 'The so-called Bavarian *fascisti* continue to hold frequent rallies,' he wrote. 'Bands of troops march about in strictly military formation. They wear grey uniforms somewhat after the Italian fashion [and] have been equipped with steel helmets of the regulation Government pattern … The reactionary press announced that the proceedings had been of a purely social and sporting character. Even allowing for the somewhat quaint ideas that still prevail as to correct sporting attire, it is difficult to believe that steel helmets, tight-fitting military uniforms, and machine gun slings are necessary for a day's sport in Bavaria.'

It was reported that the excitable leader of the organisation was prepared to grant interviews to British journalists for a fee of £5, but *The Times'* man did not think the scoop was worth the outlay. Instead he offered this sketch of the man: 'Adolf Hitler has been described recently as one of the three most dangerous men in Germany. This is probably rather a flattering estimate of the little Austrian sign painter. By many he is regarded as a useful tool, to be discarded in the case of success and disowned in the event of failure.' And sure enough, Hitler the rabble-rouser was in a Munich prison by the end of the year, having botched an attempt to overthrow the Bavarian government. The readers of *The Times* were free to assume that they had heard the first and the last of him.

BRITISH EMPIRE EXHIBITION – 1924

The Empire Exhibition at Wembley was a celebration of the great global family over which Britain ruled. Almost every imperial possession was represented by its own exotic pavilion, displaying the wares and achievements of that country. In the Ceylon pavilion the air was thick with the smell of spices. In the Canadian pavilion you could view a life-size representation of the Prince of Wales carved from refrigerated butter. Over the course of two summers, the Exhibition had 27 million visitors.

A ROYAL DAY OUT

The Exhibition opened for business on St George's Day, 1924. To mark the occasion, King George V made a speech that was broadcast live across the country, and Edward Elgar conducted an orchestra playing his best-known composition, *Land of Hope and Glory*. Queen Mary (left) was one of the first visitors; she inspected the pavilions in the company of a sizeable posse of courtiers, police officers and African tribesmen. These last were some of the hundreds of colonial subjects who had been shipped to the mother country as living exhibits: in the course of a day you could encounter Australian sheep-shearers, Ashanti weavers, Malay basketweavers – and many other artisans all hard at work. It fell to the the King's younger son, the Duke of York, later George VI (below), to sample the more frivolous pleasures on offer, such as the helter-skelter. After all, the Exhibition was not just a trade fair, it was also a vast amusement park.

ON OUR WAY TO WEMBLEY

The architectural centrepiece of the Empire Exhibition, and the first part of it to be built, was the Empire Stadium, later renamed Wembley Stadium. Its most distinctive features were its twin towers, one of which can be seen here taking shape during construction (left). The stadium was built in precisely 300 days, and was ready just four days before the first event ever staged there: the 1923 FA Cup Final between Bolton Wanderers and West Ham, which Bolton won 2–0. The game is sometimes known as the 'White Horse' final, after a white (actually a grey) police horse called Billie who helped to restore order after a pitch invasion by the crowds. By the following year, the stadium stood at the centre of an eclectic conurbation of pavilions and that year's cup final – between Aston Villa and Newcastle (below right) – served as a curtain raiser for the Exhibition as a whole.

Over the rest of the summer the stadium provided the stage for many of the exhibition's events, including a display of rodeo skills by a team of cowgirls (below left). But the real crowd-pulling attractions were the old-fashioned merry-go-rounds, the 'joy jaunts' (right), and newer-fangled rides such as the teacup-shaped bumper cars. The pavilions and all the amusements were dismantled when the Exhibition closed in 1925. The Empire Stadium itself was slated for demolition, but it was spared that fate when a far-sighted entrepreneur bought it with a down payment of £12,000. Renamed Wembley Stadium, it became the spiritual home of English football. Its twin towers, like giant salt and pepper pots, were a well-known London landmark for precisely 80 years – until they were torn down to make room for a new stadium in 2003.

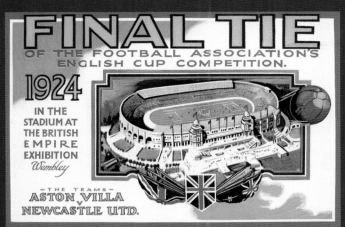

FINAL TIE
OF THE FOOTBALL ASSOCIATION'S
ENGLISH CUP COMPETITION.

1924

IN THE
STADIUM AT
THE BRITISH
EMPIRE
EXHIBITION
Wembley

— THE TEAMS —
ASTON VILLA
v
NEWCASTLE UTD.

'To stimulate trade, to strengthen bonds that bind the Mother Country to her Sister States and Daughter Nations.'

Stated aim of the British Empire Exhibition

A WOMAN'S WORLD

On the day that the Armistice was declared bringing the war to an end in November 1918, the novelist Florie Annie Steel sat down to pen an article for the *Daily Mail*. 'The world is fresh and new for womanhood', she wrote. 'It is not possible for us to go back to what we were before the flame of war tried us as in a fire. And why should we?' It was already clear to Steel, as it was to millions of other women across Britain, that the post-war world was going to be very different.

POOL PARTY The latest bathing suits on display in 1928. It is not just the fashions that are thoroughly modern; before the war, the unabashed smoking of cigarettes and application of makeup would have been very shocking things to do in public.

KEEP YOUNG AND BEAUTIFUL

One spectacular change for the better for women had come about in the hastily organised 'khaki election' of December 1918, when for the first time women were allowed to take part – both as voters and as candidates. For the suffragettes of the pre-war years, the women who had fought long and suffered mightily to win electoral rights, this was a moment to savour, but there was still more to be done. The victory was only partial since only women over 30 were granted the privilege of voting (though, oddly, a woman could stand for election as an MP at 21). All the same, the attainment of even a limited degree of female suffrage was a huge step towards formal equality with men.

Genuine electoral parity came at the end of the 1920s, when the voting age for women was lowered to 21 – the same as for men. In the ten years between those two electoral milestones women strove for equality with men in all sorts of spheres of life. Huge changes were wrought by the women of the 1920s in vital areas such as work and leisure, dress and decorum, sex and marriage. But unlike the serious-minded suffragists of the Edwardian era, this younger generation had a great deal of unabashed fun while forging their revolution.

Hairstyles and hemlines

The flapper was the dominant female archetype of the 1920s, the 'thoroughly modern miss' who was out to forget the war and have a good time. Not every woman was a flapper, of course, but most young women aspired to have something of the flapper lifestyle – or at least the flapper look. That look was, in the first instance, a spirited and determined rejection of the time-consuming and physically restrictive fashions of the pre-war era. Out went stiff whalebone corsetry and in came light clothes that allowed women to move, to bend, to play tennis and, above all, to dance. Out went long hair that took hours to comb and arrange; in came, the short, stylish and far more manageable 'bob'.

Hairstyling was no longer something that a lady had done by a servant in her private boudoir. It was now a social activity that women paid for in the public arena of a beauty salon. It followed that short hair was somehow more democratic, more egalitarian, than long hair. To cut one's hair was to demonstrate solidarity with other emancipated women. Short hair was the very cipher of modernity, and the fringed bob was just the starting point. The classic bob framed the face with two neat 'wings', à la Louise Brooks. It looked good in combination with the bell-shaped cloche hat, which became universal at the start of the Twenties and endured for a good ten years. If you wanted to wear a cloche (and everyone did), then you had to have a bob: it was impossible to pile an elaborate, old-style Grecian coiffure inside one.

SUMMER HOLIDAYS
The war's end, and the brief period of affluence and optimism that followed, presented Britain's women with some new-found and some almost forgotten freedoms. For young working-class women, like these bathers in Herne Bay (top right), there was the time and leisure for a seaside holiday. For high-born ladies such as Lady Diana Manners (bottom right) Europe was open for travel once more: she could visit old friends in Austria and strike a pose with the statuary outside their castle.

> '[There was] an almost complete rupture with pre-war ideas … an entirely new code for conduct and thought.'
> Edith, Marchioness of Londonderry, on the new relations between the sexes

The standard bob eventually gave way to the shingle, in which the back of the head was shaved. This development led to much merriment and consternation in the popular press. *Punch* ran a cartoon in which a confused young fellow was told to 'grow your hair, man, you look like a girl'. An even more extreme vogue – the 'Eton crop' – arrived in 1926. In this style the whole head of hair was cut extremely close and then slicked down to reveal the contours of the skull. Some of the most eager and bohemian exponents of the Eton crop went the whole hog and sported dinner suits and monocles, making themselves look as much like men as they possibly could. This was the logical extreme of the striving for a 'boyish' appearance that was the height of Twenties chic.

A practical statement

In some ways, the new fashions were a stylish continuation of the practical dress worn by the young women who had done war work. Long hair was a dangerous liability for women toiling over machines in arms factories, and you could not bend to milk a cow in a corset. Once the war was over, the commonsense, utilitarian changes in the outward appearance of women took on unavoidably political implications. There was a deep and universally understood link between women's social freedoms and the clothes that women actually wanted to wear. 'We are expected to walk the broad earth in that?', exclaimed one outraged young woman in response to a newspaper article that mooted a return to the long, tight,

ANYTHING MEN CAN DO
One of the themes of female emancipation in the 1920s was the constant striving on the part of women to do things that were thought of as exclusively male activities. The world of sport provided many opportunities for women to demonstrate that they were just as capable as men. These confident motorcyclists were taking part in the 1925 Six Days Reliability Trials at Brooklands. The rowers are the 1922 team from Newnham College, Cambridge – then (as now) a women-only institution.

continued on page 56

FASHION AND STYLE

The 1920s were the first decade in which fashion became the property of the young. Styles, especially for women, changed dramatically, bewildering and sometimes outraging the older generation – which, of course, was part of the point. There was a deliberate break with sartorial conventions of the past and with the buttoned-up, tight-laced attitudes that had so constricted the people of Victorian and Edwardian Britain. In the post-war world, clothes became as loose, free and frivolous as the morals (it was widely assumed) of those who wore them.

THE NEW LOOK

The change in women's clothes from before the Great War to the decade that followed it is probably the greatest ever seen in the history of fashion. In the 1920s, as in most ages, women's fashions evolved more rapidly than men's. When Cecil Beaton (far left) went to watch cricket at Lord's with his father and two sisters in 1927, the dresses worn by the women were very much of the season. In contrast, the men's morning suits were – apart from the foppish cut of Cecil's waistcoat and rakish angle of his top hat – pretty much unchanged in two generations. Women's hemlines were not quite as upwardly mobile as is often supposed. The knees were on display for a season or two in mid-decade, but generally were kept out of sight. Cloche hats, low waists and straight dresses were a consistent theme of the decade. Walking sticks (below left) seem to have been only a brief affectation for the younger generation. The woollen two-piece worn over a hip-length jumper (below right) was a popular and long-lived style, typical of the era.

'The camiknicker evolved from the camisole, which was a deep bodice which preceded the brassiere. They were fussily pretty, with a good deal of lace, and threaded with narrow ribbon, in pink or blue, called "baby ribbon".'

Ethel Edith Mannin, novelist, travel writer and 'Bright Young Thing', from *Young in the Twenties*, published in 1971

FUNDAMENTAL CHANGES

The new flapper fashions necessitated a totally new approach to underwear. Boned corsets were definitely out: sales declined by two-thirds over the course of the decade, and those who did buy them were invariably of the older generation. Younger women's undergarments, meanwhile, were reinvented almost from scratch. The most popular item was the 'camiknicker' (far left), a stitched-together word for a stitched-together combination of camisole and knickers. It was designed to be comfortable, to sit invisibly below a sleeveless, knee-length dress and to promote the bustless, hipless, almost boyish shape that was the goal of 1920s womanhood. It was often made of artificial silk, a recently invented man-made material perfectly suited to the new style since it was light, convenient and somehow heralded the future. In the 1920s women's underwear, no less than hairstyles, were an almost political statement. Camiknickers, like Eton crops and cloche hats, sent out the message that women were entitled to dress and live as they pleased. The popularity of the camiknicker inevitably led to variations on the theme, such as this combination of camisole and knee-length bloomer (left). It would not have worked so well under a short dress, and was probably designed first and foremost as a stage costume: ladies in their underwear were a stock element of light theatre in the 1920s – one of the attractions of the genre.

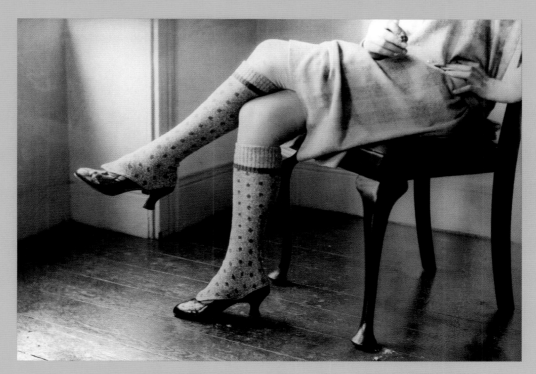

HAPPY FEET

In the Edwardian era, ladies' feet and therefore shoes were not meant to be seen. But in the fashion revolution of the 1920s, when hemlines rose from the floor and legs came into view, shoes acquired a new importance in the fashion world. This also happened to be the decade in which shoes began to be mass-produced, so suddenly there was a choice of affordable, attractive footwear to be had. A penchant lasted throughout the decade for straps fastened across the instep, and also for the elegantly curving contours of a Louis heel (top and above right). A striking piece of jewellery (above left) was one way of drawing attention to that highly prized attribute, a 'well turned ankle'. Beaded stockings, a brief vogue in 1923, achieved the same effect, but were difficult to keep straight. The knee-length 'highland puttees', tied with straps under the shoe, would help to keep out the cold in draughty country houses.

HEADS UP

Hats were an essential item of dress for women in the 1920s – and the cloche was the almost universal style. Most women had several: a change of hat was an easy and relatively cheap way to adjust one's look, particularly since most women kept their hats on when they were out in public – even in a restaurant or cinema. The vogue for hats was good news for the milliners (above), who thrived even as other businesses struggled. In Luton, the hatmaking capital of Britain, the local paper claimed that the popularity of the cloche had 'banished unemployment'. Cloches, like dresses, were subject to the fluctuations of fashion. The brim was wider some years than others; occasionally it was turned up and worn flattened against the forehead. Sometimes cloches were worn plain – in which case they bore an alarming resemblance to the scuttle helmets of the German armed forces. But they could also be adorned with a sprig of fake flowers (far left) or a jewelled brooch. Geometric Art Deco motifs were occasionally seen in ribbons and hatbands (left).

BOBS AND SHINGLES

Almost every young women cut her hair short, but there was still room to express one's own style. The actress Jessie Matthews (top) looked fabulous with her 'raven's wing' bob. The three chorus girls (top right) display the decade's predominant styles: a fringeless bob, a whole-head 'permanent wave' and a waved shingle. The new hair salons were equipped with new-fangled machines such as electric dryers (above). Hairdressing became a lucrative industry in the decade and society coiffeurs such as Antoine Cierplikowski (right) grew rich and famous.

hobbling skirts that typified the curvaceous 'Gibson Girl' look from before the war. 'Land girls, who have known the comfort of breeches, will you consent to be pinioned in this way?', she went on. 'Munitionettes, fellow war workers, all who have learned to out-distance men in the fierce race for the omnibus, will you fall back into unequal contest?' The answer to her rhetorical questions was, of course, a resounding 'no'. But despite its obvious practicality, the flapper style seemed to some to be a deliberate denial of natural femininity. Bosoms were bound tight to create the flat-chested look and the feminine contours of the figure were disguised by lowering waistlines to sit on or below the hips. The effect was to create a shape that was variously described as 'lath-like' or 'tubular'. One fashion magazine characterised voguish women in general as 'such enchanting, sexless, bosomless, hipless, thighless creatures'.

Some people tried to account for the new look by pointing to the wartime shortage of fats and sugars, as if the privation of rationing had turned an entire generation into scrawny stick insects. Some disapproving, overwhelmingly male, commentators saw the denial of hips and breasts as a symbolic and unpatriotic refusal on the part of women to embrace the maternal side of their natures. It was surely a woman's duty, went the argument, to knuckle down to the business of bearing and rearing sons to replace those who had been killed and – though this

ALL DRESSED UP
Though Britain was moving in a more egalitarian direction, there were still plenty of occasions when being posh was what mattered most. One such was the Eton versus Harrow cricket match, which was played each year at Lord's. On the day of the game the seats at the ground were occupied by the boys of the two elite schools, accompanied by their well-to-do families. These three well-dressed women on their way to the game in 1928 ooze the confidence that comes with wealth and youth – and their rather gauche schoolboy escort seems a little overwhelmed by their glamorous presence.

was not explicitly stated – to provide a new crop of cannon fodder for the next war when it came. Even high-heeled shoes were criticised on the grounds that they were anti-maternal. It was seriously suggested by some doctors that the unnatural act of walking in shoes with heels could displace a woman's uterus and so render the daughters of the Empire infertile.

None of this impressed the flappers, many of whom had lost fathers or brothers in Flanders and knew well enough what the war had cost. 'The reason my generation bobbed and shingled their hair, flattened their bosoms, and lowered their waists, was not that they wanted to be masculine, but that we didn't want to be emotional', wrote Barbara Cartland, a flapper in her youth. 'War widows, many of them still wearing crepe and widows' weeds in the Victorian tradition, had full bosoms, full skirts, and fluffed-out hair. To shingle was to cut loose from the maternal pattern; it was an anti-sentiment symbol, not an anti-feminine one.'

> 'Bobbed hair is a state of mind ... I consider getting rid of our long hair one of the many little shackles that women have cast aside in their passage to freedom.'
>
> Mary Garden, opera singer, writing in 1927

At the time, the perceived lack of femininity was the main objection to the new women's fashion. From the point of view of many men, modern girls looked wilfully unsexy. But not everyone thought so. The aesthetic eye of Cecil Beaton, just beginning to make a name for himself as a photographer, clearly saw the attraction of the new. 'To me the fashions of the twenties are infinitely alluring', he later wrote. 'One is above all struck by the simplicity of line ... those longer-than-life ladies ... symbolised the visual aspect of the period ... The 1914 war preceded an utter revolution in the concept of femininity, a revolution which, with its planes, straight lines, flattening out of bosoms and silhouettes, is more than superficially related to cubism in art, and to the tubular world of Fernand Léger.'

Legs and lingerie

Without doubt, there were exciting elements in the flapper uniform that mitigated the androgynous effect. There was the fact that dresses grew shorter in the first half of the 1920s, thereby eroticising women's legs. Pre-war dresses had encased women down to the ankle, making them look like tottering mermaids. Now, as hemlines rose, more and more leg was on show and usually it was displayed to best advantage in flesh-coloured 'artsilk' – that is 'artificial silk', the newly invented rayon. A garter worn just above the knee made for a titillating finishing touch. 'They were delicious concoctions of ribbon and rosebuds and lace', wrote Ethel Mannin, 'sometimes with a dashing touch of feather or marabout, excitingly glimpsed when the knees were crossed, and worn for no other purpose, it would seem, since our lovely shiny silk stockings were supported by suspenders.'

More alluring still was the new underwear necessitated by 1920s styles. This was of course not generally on show, but thanks to the cinema and the stage, everybody knew what went on beneath that cylindrical exterior. In a play entitled *The Garden of Eden*, the American actress Tallulah Bankhead – who represented the outrageous extreme of post-war womanhood – sensationally ripped off her wedding dress on stage to reveal the flimsy one-piece combination undergarment known as the camiknicker. Anny Ondra wore a similar garment in the first British talkie, *Blackmail*, directed by Alfred Hitchcock. She played the murderer and in the most celebrated scene stalked her victim dressed only in a short cami and armed with a large kitchen knife.

For ordinary women, the main advantage of the camiknicker over anything that had gone before was that it was loose-fitting and therefore comfortable to wear. Gone were restrictive whale-bone corsets and starched cottons. Instead, women could choose from light, silky undergarments, prettily trimmed in different colours. The writer Ethel Mannin recalled: 'The most popular shade for lingerie, as we genteelly called underclothes, was pink. The term was "prostitute pink" – but we liked it.'

LOVE AND MARRIAGE

The casual use of terms like 'prostitute pink' helped to earn flappers and their male consorts their reputation for immorality. It was widely assumed that the flamboyant and scandalous Tallulah Bankhead was not joking when she made remarks such as 'I've tried several varieties of sex. The conventional position makes me claustrophobic. And the others give me either a stiff neck or lockjaw.' The older generation feared and suspected that women who liked to charleston

HERE COMES THE BRIDE

Marriage was still the normal route to security and happiness for women of all classes. This young bride (above) on the way to her wedding is Lady Elizabeth Bowes Lyon, the future Queen Mother. When she married the Duke of York in 1923, the affection of the nation followed in her train. The confetti-covered groom with top-hat in hand (right) is Alfred Hitchcock – the very English formality of his wedding in 1926 contains no hint of the talent to terrify and shock that was just beginning to emerge in his cinema work. Shorter hemlines soon featured even on bridal gowns, as worn by this beaming bride (left). The groom was a fireman and the guard of honour was provided by his colleages.

ALL IN THE FAMILY
The almost annual round of childbirth took a heavy toll on married working-class women. The birth of triplets, like this trio known as the Edmonton Triplets (above), was an extremely rare event that made the news, but large families were very much the norm rather than the exception. Charities worked and helped in poor communities, but few people were prepared to tackle the issue of birth control, and many, like this Catholic nun (left), were from organisations adamantly opposed to any form of family planning. In her campaign to promote birth control, Marie Stopes quoted a letter she received from one barely literate woman: 'What I would like to know is how I can save having any more children as I think I have done my duty to my Country having had 13 children, 9 boys and 4 girls ... I suffer very bad with varrecross veines in my legs and my ankles gives out and I jest drops down.'

the nights away were also more than likely inclined to be sexually promiscuous, and that the licentious behaviour of the privileged few was somehow seeping out and influencing the morals of society as a whole.

Certainly mores were changing. Sex outside marriage – or more likely, in anticipation of marriage – became much more common in the Twenties than it had been in the preceding decades. This was surely one effect of the war. What was the point of waiting for marriage, when you knew that your betrothed would go away and might never return? Everybody had been aware that the death toll was creating a shortage of men and a corresponding surplus of women, and certain far-sighted individuals had also seen that this imbalance was likely to have damaging social and emotional consequences. As early as 1916, the feminist and suffragist Helena Swanwick had declared in a speech that 'when this devastating war is over there will be more young women than young men to mate with them. Are the older people who made the war and sent the young men to give their lives in it going to wash their hands of the consequences to the mateless maidens, to talk outrageously of them as "waste products of civilisation", and to offer nothing but lifelong repression?'

For years, people worried about the demographic consequences of a female 'surplus' in the population, and certainly the carnage in France deprived many individual women of the chance of marriage. But it was a myth that the imbalance between the sexes put the fruitfulness of the nation as a whole in jeopardy. Statistics show that, while the incidence of marriage decreased in the 1920s, the dip was shallow. Among younger age groups, the number of marriages actually increased. At the same time, people's vision of what a marriage should be started to shift from the Victorian ideal, in which the husband was the undisputed patriarch and ruler of the household, to something more balanced and companionable. In matters of sex, there was a dawning realisation among both middle and working classes that women had rights in the bedroom – not least, to information about sex – just as they did at the ballot box.

Pioneering family planning

Many came to this knowledge through the pioneering work of Marie Stopes, who made it her life's mission to tackle the profound sexual ignorance of British people, and of British women in particular. She published two books that were widely read in the Twenties. The first of them, *Married Love*, set out to describe the mechanics of intimacy between husband and wife (it was always husband and wife – Stopes deeply disapproved of sex outside marriage). Her aim was to instruct and to strip away the layers of shame that had accrued to the subject over the decades. Her language was lyrical and sometimes confusingly obscure, as when she set out to describe an orgasm: 'The half-swooning sense of flux which overtakes the spirit in that eternal moment at the apex of rapture sweeps into its flaming tides the whole essence of the man and woman, and, as it were, the heat of the contact vapourises their consciousness so that it fills the whole of cosmic space …' But her readers seemed to understand what she was driving at and got the gist of the message – that sexual desire was normal, that most sexual problems were solvable and that sex itself was not shameful. Many men engaged to be married wrote to her to say that they had given their fiancée a copy of her book.

Stopes's other book, *Wise Parenthood*, was about birth control. She believed that contraception was necessary to ensure that the racial stock of the imperial British remained strong and pure and, more compassionately, to prevent suffering to women – poor women, above all. The section of society that knew least about family planning was the one least able to afford to raise large families. Stopes routinely recommended that women use the 'Dutch cap', a device just then becoming widely available. But she fought a losing battle against men's unwillingness to take any responsibility for birth control. One man described the use of so-called 'male appliances' as 'like having a bath with top hat and spurs on'.

In 1921 Stopes opened Britain's first family planning clinic in Holloway, North London. For the first time, women – married women, at least – had a place to go for practical help and advice on birth control. Professional doctors – all of them men, of course – were practically useless in this regard. One woman complained that doctors were constantly telling her to have no more children, but when she asked them how to achieve this 'they just smile'. Stopes's charitable undertaking brought much criticism from churchmen – especially from Catholic ones. She sued (and lost) when a Catholic doctor accused her of 'experimenting on the poor'. But it was the gentle, sensible thoughts expressed in *Married Love* that prompted this vitriolic response from one male reader: 'Is it a desire to put bank notes into your pocket that you wrote such stuff? Do you really think that my wife and I are sadly in need of such dirty advice as you offer? Some of the things you propose in your book might have emanated from the brain of a Kaffir woman.'

A FORCE FOR CHANGE
Dr Marie Stopes (above), remembered today as a pioneering campaigner for birth control, was also a brilliant scholar, a palaeontologist and a passionate believer in women's suffrage. She is pictured here with her second husband, Humphrey Verdon Roe, outside the Royal Academy in London in 1926. Although her first marriage had ended in annulment, Stopes remained an advocate for the married state and disapproved of sex between unmarried couples.

WORKING WOMEN

Many of the men who wrote to Marie Stopes expressed concerns that it might not be proper to allow their wives to continue working after marriage. This concern was part of a wider national debate about the role of women in the workplace. There was a widespread belief that it was a bride's duty as a woman and a citizen to put aside her work to stay at home and raise children. Some skilled women workers – teachers, nurses, even sorely needed doctors – found that the decision to work or not to work was taken out of their hands by employers, many of whom sacked female employees as a matter of policy as soon as they married. Right through the decade and beyond, Establishment figures occasionally voiced the opinion that such measures constituted the obvious answer to the evil of male

GOOD MORNING, MISS
It was said ruefully in the 1920s that 'men must be educated, and women must do it'. Then, as now, women constituted a large proportion of the teaching staff in primary schools. Many of those teachers belonged to the National Union of Women Teachers, which broke away from the NUT in 1920 to campaign for equal pay with men. The NUWT addressed feminist issues such as the marriage bar and maternity rights, as well as purely educational matters such as corporal punishment, class sizes and the school leaving age.

'We know now, as we never knew before, what women can do.'

George Birmingham, novelist, writing in 1919 in praise of working women

unemployment. As late as 1933, Sir Herbert Austin, owner of the car firm and a Birmingham MP, declared that all employed women in Britain should be sacked and their positions given to jobless men.

Such views, like so many of the attitudes and prejudices of the Twenties, were rooted in the war years. While the fight was on, women were showered with praise for rolling up their sleeves and labouring in factories, driving trams, taking the place of engineers and mechanics, as well as office workers. The resilience and know-how exhibited by the female half of the population came as a surprise to many, and seemed to suggest that a new economic and social order might be one of the fruits of victory. 'Women themselves are conscious, as they never were before, of their own powers', wrote the novelist George Birmingham in 1919. 'We have everything to hope for and very little to fear from the new activities, the new powers of those who in time of trial have shown themselves noble-hearted, devoted and capable.' On the other hand, men recently returned from the front began to complain that 'the girls were clinging to their jobs, would not let go of the pocket-money which they had spent on frocks'. What had been seen as selfless toil by women while the war was on turned into selfish money-grabbing in the cash-strapped peace. Female civil servants in particular were viewed with disdain. 'While there are a quarter of a million ex-soldiers who cannot get work', commented Field Marshal Sir William Robertson, 'the retention of one woman in the War Office is a monstrous injustice.'

Longstanding suffragists such as Eleanor Rathbone, president of the National Union of Societies for Equal Citizenship, saw this kind of talk as a dangerous attack on women's rights. 'The popular outcry against the employment of women is arousing very bitter feeling among women', she wrote to *The Times*. 'To judge from these many utterances, one would imagine that women were aliens [foreigners], instead of citizens who pay their full share of taxation and have the same right as other citizens to take whatever part in the industry of the country their abilities have won for them. To shut these women out from the opportunity of earning their living is unjust to them and not, in the long run, in the interests of the country.' Surprisingly, perhaps, Field Marshal Robertson's viewpoint was shared by some well-educated, gainfully employed women, who put a noble gloss on redundancy by seeing it as a form of sacrifice. 'The present is not the time for women to press their claim to any work that can be considered a man's job',

FLOWER GIRLS

In the economy of the 1920s there were many jobs that only women were willing to do. These workers are gathering in the daffodil harvest in Cornwall. West Country farmers could make good money growing daffodils, which bloomed early in the southwest due to the mild climate. Regiments of women would cut the flowers and tie them into bundles, which were then freighted by train to market in London. Luxury items such as cut flowers would have been impossible to supply without a ready pool of cheap female labour. This springtide source of work dried up later in the century, when it became possible to import flowers earlier and even more cheaply from overseas.

A POLICEWOMAN'S LOT
The first female police officers were recruited during the Great War and by the beginning of the 1920s there were about 150 women police constables, or 'WPCs', in England and Wales. Their role was restricted – they dealt mostly with matters involving women and children. Often they were little more than uniformed secretaries, and promotion beyond the rank of constable was unheard of. Not surprisingly, few women went into the force. On the eve of the Second World War, there were still fewer than 250 policewomen in the UK.

wrote one female civil servant. 'It seems to me that it would be a national service if women should now practise a kind of self-denying ordinance and tacitly decide that for this generation they will call a halt to their efforts to increase the number of women in masculine jobs.'

All parties in this ongoing debate – men and women – made an exception for 'charwomen, shorthand typists and typists', whose work was regarded as 'non-substitutional', that is, beneath the dignity of a self-respecting war veteran. In the end it was through this kind of work, non-skilled or humbly administrative drudgery, that women began to gain a foothold in male-dominated workplaces. Clerical jobs, in particular, were a kind of Trojan horse that got women inside office buildings and made them an acceptable presence among the regiments of 'black-coated workers'. At the very bottom of the employment ladder – at the pitheads or in the mills of the north – the fact that women doing factory or manual work were paid less than men turned out to be a kind of blessing for women when, later in the decade, new waves of economic crisis swept across the

THE SERVANT PROBLEM

Many women left domestic service during the war and it proved hard to tempt them back. There was a general shortage of cooks and housemaids – this one (right) came from Austria – leading to the clichéd bourgeois complaint that 'you can't get the staff these days'. In middle-class homes, young live-in housemaids were being replaced by the 'daily' – an older women who lived locally, helped around the house and went home at the end of the day. It was beginning to be clear that the lives of women would be different in future, but girls still had to be prepared to take on the domestic duties. These urban schoolgirls (below) are being taught the right way to set a table. The housewives of the future would be largely doing their own cooking and cleaning, with some help from new 'labour-saving' devices such as vacuum cleaners and electric stoves. There was still a sense that the preparation of food was a menial task that should not be observed by visitors, so in the newest homes kitchens were tucked away at the back of the house.

country. Higher-paid men were often the first to be given their cards, while cheaper female labour was kept on. In working-class communities, this pattern tended to raise the status of women within the family, as often the young women of the household continued to bring home a wage after their brothers and fathers had been laid off. In this way, the women of the Twenties gradually took possession of what the writer Vera Brittain described in 1927 as 'the twentieth century's greatest gift to women. It is dignified work', she wrote, 'which puts her on the same level as men.'

Brittain was perhaps overstating the case, because women were still a long way from achieving equality with men in the workplace. The Sex Disqualification (Removal) Act, passed in 1919, was a step in the right direction. It stated unequivocally that: 'A person shall not be disqualified by sex or marriage from the exercise of any public function, or from being appointed to or holding any civil or judicial office or post, or from entering or assuming or carrying on any civil profession or vocation ...'. This meant that qualified women could come knocking on the door of certain male bastions, and that the professional men on the inside were legally obliged to let them in. The effect of the new law was felt most strongly in the legal profession itself. In 1921, Ivy Williams made history by becoming the first women to be called to the Bar in England. She had passed all her law examinations by 1903, but had to wait for the change in the law before

A DESK OF ONE'S OWN
Training as a nurse (right) was already a time-honoured career path for women. It required intelligence, as well as the feminine virtue of compassion, and so commanded respect. Office work was a newer option; the young woman above is at her desk in the Topical Press Agency in 1924. Women clerks were not always treated seriously. According to the *Daily Mail* in 1927, they 'kept their position partly, if not chiefly, by their appearance'. *Miss Modern*, a magazine aimed at female office workers, explained to its readers exactly why their looks were so important: 'A pretty, charmingly turned-out secretary is a great asset to a busy man. Being pretty she has confidence in herself, and so is more self-reliant than a plain girl. Also she adds brightness to an office and helps give it a cheerful atmosphere.'

she was allowed to practise her chosen profession. She then chose not to do so, and so the honour of being the first working female barrister fell to Helena Normanton in 1922. Normanton was subsequently one of the first two women to be appointed King's Counsel, and has the small distinction of being the first woman ever to be issued a British passport in her maiden name.

A long list of female firsts

One curious consequence of the Sex Disqualification Act was that Britain became obsessed with female pioneers. It was always news when a woman did something that a woman had never done before. The first female 'stable lad' made her debut with much media fanfare in 1919. Not long after came the first women jurors and the first female boxers. More spectacularly, Lady Mary Bailey set the world altitude record for light aeroplanes by climbing to 18,000 feet in a flimsy de Havilland Moth; nobody of either sex had flown that high. Lady Bailey had earned her pilot's certificate the year before, having taken lessons in secret from her husband as a way to 'get away from prams'. Before the decade was out, she cemented her reputation as a pioneering pilot – or 'aviatrix', as the newspapers

COMMUNAL LABOUR
The hats sported by these women are not some strange form of national dress, but the typical headgear of Covent Garden workers. These women are shelling peas during the porterage strike that hit the fruit and vegetable market in August 1924. The height of summer was the busiest time of year for the market, and male porters could earn up to £9 a week. Wholesalers and retailers thought the cost was too high, the porters themselves thought it was too low, and a month-long stoppage ensued. There is no knowing what these women were paid, but it would certainly have been much less than a unionised male worker would have expected for the same job.

'WHEN THE BOAT COMES IN'
A cheerful young Scottish woman gutting herrings at Great Yarmouth in 1926. Much of the work open to women was seasonal and migrational in character. Thousands of women of all ages travelled from Scotland to Great Yarmouth for the herring season each autumn. There they did the messy job of processing the catch and salting it in barrels. They would work intensely, in the open air, whenever the fishing boats came in. Between times, they sat in groups around the harbour – knitting, chatting in their northern brogue and waiting for the trawlers to arrive with the catch.

called women flyers – by flying solo from England to South Africa. She was equipped with a small map taken from a travel agent's advertisement, and a revolver in case she ran into trouble with 'tribesmen'.

A less spectacular, but in the long run more significant achievement, belongs to Margaret Bondfield, who was appointed Minister of Labour in Ramsay MacDonald's Cabinet in 1929 and so became the first female member of government. On the day she and her male colleagues took the train to Windsor to be sworn in by the King 'there were crowds all along the line cheering, and engine drivers blowing whistles as our trains came through'. Since no woman had ever taken part in the ceremony before, no-one knew the protocol. Should she wear a hat? Miss Bondfield decided not, as a wide brim might scratch His Majesty's nose when she bowed to kiss the royal hand.

Margaret Bondfield had been an MP since 1923 – she was one of the first women to win a seat for the Labour Party – and was an eloquent parliamentary spokeswoman for women's rights. One of her colleagues on the Labour benches was Ellen Wilkinson, who became known as 'Red Ellen' for her radical politics and her auburn hair. Looking back on the decade from the start of the Thirties,

YOU SHALL GO TO THE BALLOT
Women had plenty of opportunities to exercise their newly acquired right to vote: there were no fewer than four general elections over the course of the decade. But the political parties were unsure of how to appeal to women – and in any case it was widely assumed that wives would dutifully vote the same way as their husbands. Politicians could not help describing female voters condescendingly as 'domestic chancellors' whenever the economy was under discussion. The voting age for women was lowered to 21 in 1928, and some commentators predicted unseemly dizziness at the ballot box. But according to the *Daily Express*, in the 'flapper election' of 1929 'the women went about the business of voting solemnly, responsibly and thoroughly'.

HEROINE OF SUFFRAGE
Eleanor Rathbone (on the left) was a campaigner for votes for women who carried her zeal and enthusiams into the era of women's suffrage. In 1919 she became president of the National Union of Women's Suffrage Societies. Since the vote had by now been won, the NUWSS under Rathbone's leadership was renamed the National Union of Societies for Equal Citizenship, and set about the task of challenging discrimination against women in other areas of life. Rathbone argued that married women were forced into a kind of economic oppression by the fact that the family's income always passed first through the hand of the husband. From this conviction arose her most enduring idea, that wives should be paid a 'family allowance' by the state. She argued the case with those who objected to 'throwing the financial burden of bringing up children on the national exchequer' – and won. Rathbone became an MP in 1929.

Wilkinson noted that 'women doing startling new things fill the papers until one begins to wonder if men are doing anything at all. They beat flying records, carry off the architectural prize of the year, apparently beating men at their own games all along the line. The impression gets about that all England's women are barristers, or aeronauts, or crack Channel swimmers.' She went on: 'Of course, it is not like that really.' But it was not entirely unlike that either. Individually and collectively women achieved great things in the Twenties – far more than the pre-war generation could have hoped for or expected. All in all, not bad going for a bunch of dizzy flappers.

FIRST FEMALE MINISTER
Margaret Bondfield (right), the first woman to become a member of the British Cabinet. Her appointment led to a departure from the usual royal protocol, when she and the other new government ministers were presented to the King. 'Each of us in turn went forward to kneel on the King's footstool, holding out the right arm,' she later recorded. 'By ancient tradition this ceremony is acted in silence, but when my turn came King George broke the customary silence to say "I am pleased to be the one to whom has come the opportunity to receive the first woman Privy Councillor".' She described the mixture of pride and humility she felt in that moment. 'Pride that I should be called upon to occupy this niche in history; humility in the certain knowledge that uncounted numbers of pioneers had a greater right to it.'

TOWN AND COUNTRY RICH AND POOR

For countless generations, to be wealthy meant to own land – to own the agricultural products of the land, to be lord over the people who lived on the land and, in more recent centuries, to have the right to exploit the coal and minerals that lay beneath the soil. For some, like the left-wing political thinker Sidney Webb, this was a situation in desperate need of change. 'Nine-tenths of all the accumulated wealth belongs to one-tenth of the population', he wrote in 1920. 'The continued existence of the functionless rich, of persons who deliberately live by owning instead of by working, adds insult to injury.'

PUPPIES FROM HEAVEN The Honourable Mrs Chesterman enjoys a day out at a Northampton Aero Club meeting in 1929. She is holding aloft two stuffed toy dogs, dropped by parachute as part of the display; the dog on the lead is real.

INHERITED WEALTH

The kind of privileged people that Webb had in mind included families such as the Londonderrys. They owned 50,000 acres of land across England, Ireland and Wales, and were proprietors of coalfields in County Durham that employed 10,000 men. Lady Londonderry, granddaughter of the Duke of Sutherland and wife of the seventh marquess of Londonderry, used her immense wealth to gain access to political power. She held a grand reception to mark each new session of Parliament, which the prime minister of the day invariably attended with all his Cabinet. These occasions were as much a part of the British political system as the Budget or the King's Speech. Even Ramsay MacDonald, the first Labour Prime Minister – who, as a socialist, might have been expected to shun upper-class ostentation – was in thrall to Lady Londonderry during his time in office. She was his closest friend and confidante. For many class-conscious Labour supporters, it was less Lady Londonderry's unearned eminence that rankled than MacDonald's readiness to cosy up to her.

Title to the land

Lady Londonderry was a fixture of political life well into the 1930s. Yet in 1920, the year that Sidney Webb published his hefty socialist tome, *A Constitution for the Socialist Commonwealth of Great Britain*, the wealth and power of the landed gentry was already on the wane. The changes in fortune that took place over the decade were due not so much to the rise of socialism, as to the vagaries of capitalism. In particular, the land-owning aristocracy were under siege from a relatively new tax on inherited wealth. In 1908 death duties – or estate duty, as it was then known – were raised from a fairly negligible rate to 8 per cent on any inheritance worth a million pounds or more. The introduction of expensive social policies – and the even costlier war – encouraged governments to hike up estate duty at every turn, so by 1918 the rate stood at 30 per cent.

Most of that taxable wealth was tied up in the land itself and the elder sons of the aristocracy, bequeathed their estates by their fathers, often had to sell some of their land in order to keep the rest of it. Some of those sons and heirs were themselves killed in the war. Quite apart from the dynastic implications for old aristocratic families, the economic effects of the premature death of an eldest son could be crippling; if he had already inherited the estate, it would

KING COAL
King Alfonso XIII of Spain, flanked by Lord and Lady Londonderry, on a visit to a new colliery in Seaham, County Durham, in about 1925 (bottom left). The Marquess refused to countenance any compromise with his workers when they demanded better pay and conditions. Around the time that this picture was taken, he said 'I am proposing to devote a great deal of my time to defeating the socialist menace in one of the reddest portions of the kingdom' – meaning his own coalfields in the northeast.

'There is still an Upper Class … [who] wield a certain influence behind the scenes'

Lady Londonderry, writing in 1938

LADY OF THE HOUSE
The Astor family at home. Lady Nancy Astor became the first woman to take a seat in the House of Commons, after being elected as MP for Plymouth Sutton in 1919. She was the only female MP in that Parliament. Her pioneering achievement made her an eminent public figure throughout the 1920s, but unlike many of the earliest women MPs, she had not earned her spurs in the suffrage movement. An American by birth, she was independently wealthy and led the life of an upper-class socialite. Significantly, the parliamentary seat that she won had just been vacated by her husband, Waldorf Astor, who had been elevated to the Lords.

RURAL PURSUITS
A competitor leads his prize bull at the Royal Counties Agricultural Show in Guildford, Surrey, in 1922. The three young ladies on the right, from the East Anglian Institute of Agriculture, have their hands full with young charges for sale at the Essex Pig Show in Chelmsford in 1927. Although most land was in the hands of large landowners, a large proportion of the rural population were not so much farmers as smallholders – people who eked out a living from a few acres of rented land. Much of the smallholding would be devoted to growing vegetables, but there might also be a small apple orchard and a chicken run. Most smallholders would invest in a pig in spring, to be killed in the autumn and provide a valuable source of protein through the winter. Pigs were cheap to rear, because they could be fed on scraps and windfall apples. Other necessities could be had by barter, but for most families, some sort of extra paid work would be necessary to avoid dire poverty. Those that owned cows could let them graze freely on the roadside verges – a practice that became more hazardous, and so less common, with the rise of the motor car.

mean paying death duties twice in one generation. This was often enough to sever the long-standing connections between noble families and their ancestral lands.

At the same time, the value of agricultural land was falling – a process that had begun back in Victorian times. After the war, a point was reached where the interest on money in the bank was giving a better return than could be earned from the rents and produce of the land. Consequently many families sold the houses and lands that they had owned for generations, and bought into bonds, stocks and equities (a strategy that some came to regret bitterly at the end of the decade, when the global stock market crumbled to dust). For a short while, there was no shortage of buyers for country estates. The new breed of industrialists – some of them MPs, described by Stanley Baldwin, before becoming Prime Minister, as 'hard-faced men who look as if they had done very well out of the war' – were only too keen to acquire the prestige of a stately pile. Many of them already had the requisite title – or soon would, thanks to Lloyd George's dubious policy of selling peerages for cash. The result of all these trends was a massive shift in ownership of the countryside. It has been said that more land changed hands in the Twenties and Thirties than at any time since the Norman Conquest.

This process entailed a parallel social upheaval for the English aristocracy. One way to keep the old estates together was to marry money rather than sell to it. That meant admitting the nouveaux riches to aristocratic society, and ultimately,

'The bottom's coming up, my dear, and the top's coming down.'
Overheard remark of an anonymous aristocratic lady

perhaps, into one's own family and bloodline. Some of the most influential hostesses and sought-after heiresses of the Twenties were Americans who had grown wealthy in business – charming families such as the Astors, the Cunards and the Vanderbilts. They were not just super-rich, they were also a breath of fresh air. They carried the heady scent of the Jazz Age with them like pollen on a bee. And their accents, being foreign, did not grate on the ear or betoken less than impeccable class origins.

POOR MAN, BEGGAR MAN

Beyond the large imposing doors of Berkeley or Eaton Square, on the streets of every city, there were destitute and damaged ex-servicemen looking for odd jobs, or standing in the gutters singing patriotic songs with a cap at their feet. Even before the slump set in 1921, the slogan 'Homes For Heroes' sounded very hollow. A good proportion of heroes' homes were in fact slums of unbelievable squalor. 'Here we have a population of some 30,000 packed into a fetid

BAREFOOT ON THE COBBLES
This cheerful group of children were photographed outside their homes in Belfast in 1926. Unlike impoverished rural families, the urban poor had to find the cash to buy everything they needed – every scrap of food that they ate, every item of clothing they wore. During the week many children subsisted on bread and margarine, or bread and dripping (bread was usually home-baked, in a brick oven, because that was cheaper than buying it from a shop). Protein came in the form of a slice of saveloy or the occasional egg. In many cities, communities were bound by family ties, with grandparents, cousins, aunts and in-laws all living within a street or two of each other. In other words, city slums were often urban villages, as close-knit and inward-looking as any rustic hamlet.

atmosphere arising from the excrementary deposits outside their larder windows of all this pitiful population', wrote one Northumberland man in a letter to Marie Stopes in the early Twenties. 'Vermin fill the electric light fittings in some dens like a solid block, and the walls appear to have a pattern which is composed of squashed bugs in hundreds, beds and floors urine saturated. Children are more like so many imps, filthy in mind and body, and on a dark night you can fall over big girls squatting in the road (beastly bogs rather) not altogether because they are so brought up but through the so-called ash pits having too many adult users. It is nothing for them to take a tea mug off the table, hand it to a child, and then fling urine anywhere, and put it back on the table again for tea.'

Matters were barely any better in the countryside. Overcrowding was a fact of rural life – partly because farm work, being casual and seasonal, required a peripatetic army of manual labourers. 'Families with insufficient room for themselves are under great pressure to take in lodgers', wrote a correspondent of *John Bull* magazine in 1925, 'generally young or middle-aged men who have work in the village but have no chance of getting a cottage or even a single room to themselves. Instances are legion in which these lodgers sleep in the same room with various members of the family, more or less independent of considerations of age and sex. It would serve no good purpose to give examples of the indecencies, not to say scandals, that result.' The same writer went on to discuss the standards of hygiene in country communities, which he suggested were pre-medieval. 'It is usually supposed that village life in England is much superior to town life on certain most vital concerns – especially in health and morals. In some respects the countryman today is worse off than he was in the 13th century. They were then careful of their teeth, and were in the habit of cleaning them with twigs of trees from which the bark was freshly pulled. Today the toothbrush is scarcely known.'

Making ends meet

Part of the problem in the countryside was that the long-term depression in agriculture was producing a trickle-down reduction in wages. An agricultural labourer who earned £2 a week in 1918 could only hope to take home 25 shillings (£1.25p) in 1923. This ought to have benefited the employers – the farmers who needed to employ extra hands in the busy summer months. But arable crops simply could not be made to pay. Some farmers switched to dairy in the hope that there was more money in milk than wheat. Others sat tight and hoped to ride out the economic downturn.

One farmer's wife, a Mrs Crabtree, recalled the desperate measures they were forced to adopt: 'Our worst experience of the depression was when we were faced with two months and no money coming in whatsoever. We were employing five men and they needed their wages on the Friday night, and to us those men were friends as well as our workers. My husband had in those days two beautiful Cleveland bay horses; they were the first to go, and we lived on the proceeds of them and paid our wages for the first month. Then came the second month … My husband said to me: "I can't pay the wages; what are we to do?" And I suddenly remembered we had up in the attic quite a lot of silver which had been given to us as wedding presents. We filled the back of our old Wolseley car and, believe me, it was the hardest day's work I've ever done to sell that silver to raise the wages …'

PLOUGHING A STRAIGHT FURROW
Mechanical tractors were by no means a common sight in the Twenties. Most of the power on farms was still provided by horses, and most agricultural equipment, such as the harrow used for raking the surface of the soil, was horse-drawn. Ploughing was a particularly skilled task that demanded close cooperation between the ploughman and his horses. The plough itself was by now made of materials forged in the white heat of the industrial revolution, but the skill and technique required on the part of the ploughman was unchanged since medieval times. This team (below) are competing in the horse-drawn ploughing competition at the Chertsey Agricultural Show in October 1923.

FAREWELL TO THE ISLES

LEAVING HOME

In 1923 and 1924 a catastrophic triple economic crisis struck the islands of the Hebrides. First, there was a failure of the potato crop; then the very wet summer prevented the peat harvest from taking place; and finally the normally rich herring-fishing industry was badly hit by the loss of German and Russian markets. In the midst of these disasters, Canadian agents came to the islands to encourage people to emigrate to 'a land of prosperous communities, with boundless opportunites for youth and ambition'. Many families, like the sad but determined-looking women above, decided that their best chance was to grasp the opportunity and leave. Most chose to stay, but crowded the quaysides to wave goodbye to their friends, relatives and neighbours (right).

'There is absolutely no employment of any kind for the thousands of men who are involuntarily idle.'

From an article published in 1924 in *Press & Journal*,
a pro-emigration local newspaper in the Hebrides

MIDDLE-CLASS SPREAD

Between the extremes of rich and poor stood the vast bulwark of the middle classes. Then, as now, the term covered a broad range of attitudes, occupations and circumstances. At the bottom end of the scale it encompassed teenage clerks and female typists, first-generation members of the urban bourgeoisie, doing newly invented jobs, and using their wits and earning power to escape a life of servant drudgery or manual labour. At the upper end, the middle classes included well-off professionals such as bankers and lawyers, diplomats and civil servants. Ranged between were farm-owners and country doctors, teachers and skilled tradesmen, university graduates, down-at-heel former officers and myriad small businessmen – the employers of those 'black-coated workers', as office employees were known, perched two or three rungs from the bottom of the social ladder.

NEW ROADS AND HOUSES

Two proud roadbuilders, foreman F H Atkins and workmen's representative W H Goring, wait to be presented to the Prince of Wales at the opening of the new Dartford bypass (below). New roads brought with them new housing, as speculative builders threw up middle-class homes along the highways into the big cities. The roads made it easy to get into town by car, and the proliferation of cars led in turn to the construction of more roads, then still more homes. The biggest project of all was the 'cottage estate' built over a period of ten years at Becontree near Dagenham (right, under construction). The Becontree estate, built on land compulsorily purchased from market gardeners and farmers in Essex, was paid for by London County Council. Some 25,000 small family houses were built, and more than 100,000 people – most from London's East End – moved into them. It was a hugely ambitious project and even today Becontree remains the largest housing estate in Europe.

Within this disparity there were many gradations of status – which is what George Orwell was referring to when he jokingly described his own background as 'lower upper middle class'. One thing – perhaps the only thing – that all middle-class people had in common was aspiration: they were all striving to be better off than their parents had been, and to make sure that their children did better still.

The march of suburbia

The middle-class home was the main expression of a family's status and their social hopes and fears. In the Twenties, a new kind of dwelling burst forth in large numbers, like daffodils in spring. This was the semi-detached house, two conjoined mirror-image homes, two storeys high, designed to be bought and lived in by people who, to echo Orwell, might have been termed 'middle middle middle class'. Newly constructed semis were more affordable than a free-standing house and easier to manage without servants.

Aesthetically, with their false half-timbered gables and private lawned rear gardens, they represented a backward-looking architecture that was easily mocked. Osbert Lancaster called it 'Wimbledon Transitional' or 'Stockbroker Tudor', 'a glorified version of Anne Hathaway's cottage

A NEWER LOOK
By the end of the 1920s, the Art Deco style was as ubiquitous as the cloche hat. Art Deco worked best in new settings – in new apartments and cube-like houses with flat façades, clean lines and plain interior walls that functioned like a blank canvas. Done well, the style was sophisticated and witty, but it could just as easily be conspicuously garish. The huge, dizzying diamond shapes in the scheme above make for a rather uneasy contrast with the decorative wrought ironwork of the Victorian staircase.

with such modifications as were necessary to conform to transatlantic standards of plumbing'. But the attraction of these 'olde-worlde' new-builds – apart from mod cons such as hot water and electricity – was that they placed the owner mid-way between town and country, just as the owner's fiscal status put him at the mid-point between insouciant wealth and indigent poverty. The new houses were neither too cheap nor too expensive, neither grimly urban nor inconveniently rustic. And therein lay their appeal: they were middling in every way.

Jacobethan houses – the term was coined by John Betjeman in the Thirties – were built in their thousands on the fringes of London and other cities, and throughout the home counties. For better or worse, they became the archetypal suburban style of the twentieth century. But the kind of speculative building that created the suburbs turned uglier when it stretched far out into the countryside, giving rise to the particular phenomenon known as 'ribbon development'. Throughout the Twenties and into the Thirties, speculators bought up land along highways leading into cities. They would build a string of semis or low-lying pebble-dashed bungalows on either side of the road as far as they could afford. Such houses were immensely convenient if you owned a car – as soon as you left your driveway you were bowling down the road – and they were also extremely desirable, because at the back they afforded views over open country. Here again was that perfect synthesis: easy access to the city combined with the rural idyll. But the unfortunate effect of this pattern of building was to cut travellers off from the country through which they were moving. For mile after mile, there was nothing to see but other people's neatly clipped privet hedges.

The dangers of uncontrolled speculative building had been noted by the end of the decade: 'It is no exaggeration to say that in fifty years, at the rate so-called improvements are being made, the destruction of all the beauty and charm with which our ancestors enhanced their towns and villages will be complete.' This was no snobbish architect speaking, but the Prime Minister, Stanley Baldwin, in 1928. By then, the rolling hills at the back of the original ribbon homes were themselves being built on, creating bundles of indifferent housing like varicose veins on the landscape. Some professionals believed that Baldwin's nightmare vision was already coming true. 'Take Peacehaven or Waterlooville or Bournemouth', wrote architect Clough Williams-Ellis, also in 1928. 'There was no attempt at intelligent general layout plan; all was cut-throat grab, exploitation and waste – a mad game of beggar-my-neighbour between a host of greedy little sneak-builders and speculators, supplying the demand for homes meanly and usuriously.' He was equally scornful of the houses: 'There they are – caught all higgledy-piggledy and looking thoroughly lost and foolish, indeed not knowing which way to look. "Mon Abri" stares vacantly at the shameful hinder parts of "Loch Lomond", which in turn is overlooked by the baleful scowl of "Kia-Ora" on its flank.'

Modern moments

Occasionally, in the midst of the kinds of houses that Williams-Ellis so plainly detested, one might encounter something uncompromisingly Modernist, a 20th-century house built for a 20th-century lifestyle. It is questionable how far these chic Art Deco white boxes, with their metal-framed windows and flat roofs, were suited to the English climate – which is one reason why they were often sited on the sunny south coast. To some, they were more of an eyesore than the ubiquitous semi-detached, but to others they were the concrete expression of the Twenties spirit – as racy, daring, and radical as a woman in black tie and dinner suit. And

PUBLIC DECOR
Art Deco worked well in public buildings, where there was room for a bold architectural statement. Many of the picture palaces built in the late 1920s used Deco design to great effect. The geometrically patterned floor of the Brixton Astoria (top) is typical – though the rest of the scheme is rather eclectic. In the late 1920s there was a fad for figurines, usually as decorative ornaments around the home, but also as car mascots (above). Stylised female figures and animals were favourite motifs, and in their midst the devil cocking a snook looks like an aberration.

CARTER DISCOVERS TUTANKHAMUN'S TOMB

In November 1922 the British Egyptologist Howard Carter (left) made the most sensational archaeological discovery of the 1920s – indeed of the entire 20th century. He had been working in the Valley of the Kings for several seasons without any significant breakthrough and was on the point of abandoning the dig when his water boy found the steps that led down to Tutankhamun's tomb. He immediately wired his sponsor Lord Carnarvon, who came straight out to Egypt with his daughter Evelyn – the pair are shown flanking Carter in the centre of picture below. On 26 November, 1922, Carter broke the seal on the door of the tomb. Behind him, Lord Carnarvon could not contain his excitement. 'Can you see anything?' he called. 'Yes', replied Carter, 'wonderful things.' Carter shrewdly negotiated the rights to print photographs of those things. Over the next few years, as the tomb's treasures were catalogued and brought out into the light of day, colour illustrations appeared regularly in the *Illustrated London News*. They created a vogue for all things Egyptian that influenced fashion, architecture and jewellery design well into the Thirties.

if you could not have the Art Deco exterior, you could create the look indoors, as Ethel Mannin wrote of the décor in her quaint country cottage: 'Furniture and clocks and fireplaces were all cubistic, angular, and carpets and cushions and lampshades patterned with zigzag, jazz designs. Curves were out and angles were in. There were orange cushion covers with black cats appliqued to them; there were orange and yellow artificial chrysanthemums and bright blue lupins, ideal for standing in a tall papier-mache vase in a corner of the dance room.'

Sunday drivers

Conformists and Bohemians alike took advantage of the private motor car, a social and technological development without which modern living would not have been possible. It was the growing availability of cars that made it viable for developers to sell homes in suburbs and ribbon developments, and it was the car that carried city dwellers on their Sunday voyages of exploration. In the Twenties middle-class motoring, like middle-class housing, was a way of integrating urban life with the rustic idyll. Car manufacturers understood this well, and the lure of the countryside was often the central plank of their sales pitch. 'Every weekend a holiday', ran one newspaper advertisement. 'Where shall it be this week? Through highways to old world towns and villages or byways to the woods and fields; a quick straight run to the silvery sea or a dawdle amid hills and dales. Each weekend a new scene – that is what this Standard Light Car means to the family.'

'Two years ago the lowest-price Morris sold at £465. Today we are marketing a better car at £225 complete.'

William Morris, car manufacturer, 1922

That car cost £235 in 1924, and most family machines – the Austin Sevens, the American Fords, the Talbots and the Morrises – cost about the same. By 1929 a brand-new Morris Cowley could be had for as little as £195. Such prices put a car well within the means of a professional man, whereas before the war a motor was exclusively a rich man's toy. At the end of the decade most middle-class families had a car in the garage, as surely as they had a wireless in the sitting room and roses in the back garden.

A private car was more than a means of transport, it was also an all-consuming hobby. Just mastering the controls involved a considerable commitment of time and effort. Every gear change, for example, required the driver to 'double de-clutch', which involved judging the engine speed and split-second timing. The sparsity of wayside garages meant that weekend drivers needed to be reasonable mechanics. At the very least, they had to know how to change a wheel or deal with an overheated radiator (a common problem on long uphill stretches). And they had to be strong enough to crank the engine into life with the starting handle. Unsurprisingly, independent women drivers were a rare breed.

But drivers in general were becoming ever more common. A visitor to London in 1929 would have encountered four times as many petrol-driven vehicles as horse-drawn ones. The change in the composition of urban traffic was certainly a result of the affordability of cars, but it also had something to do with the fact that cars were an exhilarating and liberating symbol of the age. The Twenties were a decade when for many Britons excitement and freedom were what life was about. A new world of pleasure was there to be had, if you wanted it and could afford it. All you had to do was reach out and grasp it.

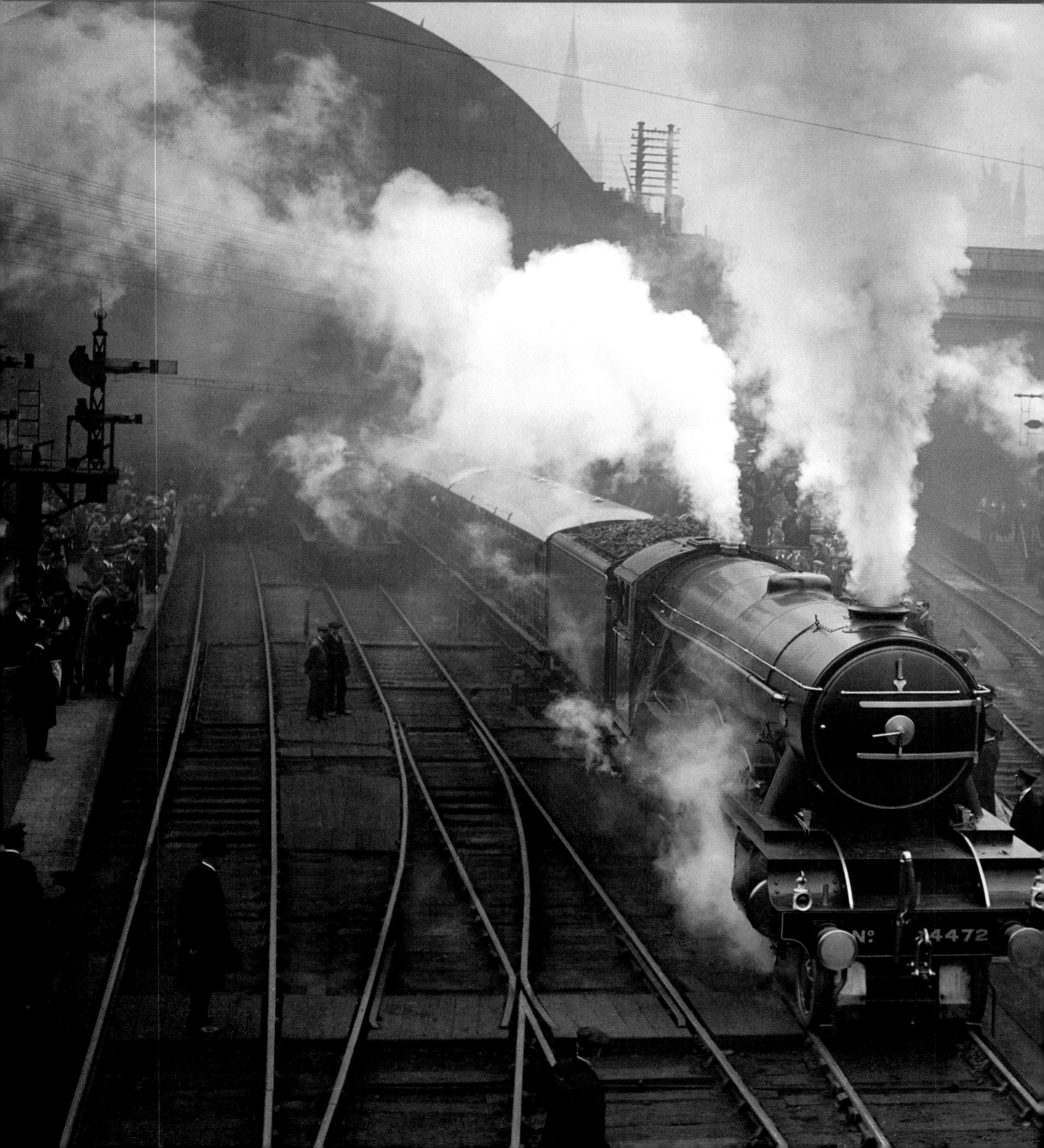
Nº 4472

TRANSPORT

In the 1920s the business of getting from one place to another became not just more democratic but also more glamorous. Personal means of transport, such as the car and the motorcycle, were now within the grasp of middle-class professionals and working-class wage-earners. Meanwhile, long-distance forms of transport – trains, ships and aircraft – aimed to offer well-to-do passengers a touch of luxury. It was, in many ways, the golden decade of travel.

STYLE ON THE MOVE
The Flying Scotsman (left) on its first non-stop run from London to Edinburgh on 11 May, 1928. The famous steam train started service on the 392-mile route in 1923. By 1928 technical improvements to the engine made it possible for the train to cover the distance on one tender of coal and arrive in Edinburgh shortly after six in the evening. A corridor was installed in the tender so that the crew could be relieved half-way without stopping the train. Steam trains were a stylish mode of travel – this one had a cocktail bar and hairdressing salon on board – but motorbikes were also chic in their way. They were a symbol of independence for flappers and the perfect way to arrive at a tennis party.

BY AIR AND BY SEA

There was an obsession in the 1920s with setting new records for speed and endurance in various forms of transport. Aeroplanes – still very much a new-fangled invention – provided plenty of scope for pioneers to test themselves and their machines. In 1926, for example, a British aviator named Alan Cobham flew to Australia and back. Here he is (top left) in the final seconds of his journey, stopping the traffic on Westminster Bridge as he comes in to land on the Thames. In 1928, in a novel test of speed, an Imperial Airways bi-plane named 'The City of Glasgow' raced the Flying Scotsman from London to Edinburgh. The plane is seen here (bottom left) crossing the river at Berwick-upon-Tweed; the train on the viaduct is not, in fact, the Flying Scotsman, but the Junior Scotsman.

Intercontinental travel was still the realm of ocean liners, such as the *Laconia* (above), seen here leaving Liverpool for New York in 1922. For a while it seemed that airships might constitute a commercial rival to seaborne carriers. The dining room of the R100 (right), which made its maiden flight in 1929, was as sumptuous as that of any ocean liner and the airship was capable of crossing the Atlantic. But in 1930 its sister ship, the R101, crashed in bad weather in northern France, bursting into flames and killing most of those on board. The development of airships in Britain thus came to an abrupt end.

ENGINE OF PROGRESS
By the end of the 1920s, cars were big business and trade car shows were a regular event at Olympia in London; this one (above) took place in 1929. The most successful British manufacturer was William Morris, a brilliant entrepreneur who got into the motorcar business as early as 1910, and exhibited his first model – the Morris Oxford – in 1912. He produced cars in large volumes on a production line at his factory at Cowley in Oxford (bottom right), and models such as the Morris Cowley led the way in affordability, forcing other car manufacturers to lower their prices, too. In many ways, Morris was the Henry Ford of the British automobile industry. Over the decade the country was opened up to motorists. The two ladies admiring Crummock Water in the Lake District (top right), may have been taking a chance on the reliability of their machine when they drove to such a remote spot, but by 1929 – when this photograph was taken – the risk was small and the stunning views were well worth it.

'How swift and yet how safe! How easily they thread the traffic, how tenaciously they take the corners, how effortlessly they top the rise!'

From a newspaper advertisement for Riley cars

LET'S DO IT

The Twenties was a decade of more or less unrestrained hedonism because having fun was a good way to forget. For a short while the British went out of their way to dance, drink and be merry, for yesterday so many had died. Pleasure in all its forms seemed a life-affirming pursuit, and for a while many people had the means to pursue it. 'For a time officers and men who had taken their war gratuities had money to burn', wrote war correspondent Philip Gibbs. 'They burned it in nightclubs and dance-halls, which sprang up like mushrooms … It was a kind of feverish gaiety which burned high and burned low. Those who went in search of joy found often an intolerable boredom. In the wild Twenties there was, now and then, an underlying depression.' At the time few people were perceptive enough to hear that note of sad despair: it was drowned out by the raucous, brassy beat of the Jazz Age.

PARTY TIME Revellers on their way to the 'motor carnival ball', one of them mounted on a sidecar that's apparently disguised as a giant cocktail shaker. All in all, a typically risqué 1920s combination of larky girls, noisy fun, silly costumes and motorised transport.

BRIGHT YOUNG THINGS

At the vanguard of the pleasure-seeking masses was a small coterie of the super-rich, well-connected men and women who became known as the Bright Young Things (BYTs). Their *raison d'être* in post-war life was to be outrageous, and their antics, as reported in the papers, provided delicious thrills of amusement or disapproval for the rest of the population. While the country reeled from crisis to crisis, they drank cocktails with amusing names such as 'Strike's Off', a coinage that really says it all about their sense of humour and the depth of their political awareness.

FANCY DRESSERS

The 'bright young things' had a rather childish fondness for dressing up. The icily beautiful Lady Castlerosse (left) wore this elaborate constellation of stars on her head for the Galaxy Ball Pageant in 1929, while the coterie of upper-class clowns (right) are enjoying the Chelsea Arts Ball from the vantage point of a box at the Royal Albert Hall. The high-pitched excitement of such occasions was captured by the socialite Duff Cooper, when he described a party at Lady Curzon's residence: 'Everyone was in the highest spirits, everyone was in fancy dress and several wore one or two different ones during the course of the evening. The stately rooms of Carlton House Terrace looked more like a Montmartre restaurant, littered with confetti, masks, streamers, celluloid balls etc. I wore first a skeleton mask in which nobody recognised me and I had the greatest fun. When I finally had to take it off to drink I later put on another different one and again escaped recognition for a long time. All the women looked beautiful, or so I thought.'

But even amid the pranks and gaiety, there was a strict social code. 'Our morals might be nowhere, but when it came to fashion and etiquette we conformed', observed Ethel Mannin. 'There were various small niceties, too – we always offered both Turkish and Virginian cigarettes when we entertained, we served finger-bowls with warm water and a slice of lemon, our coffee sugar was coloured crystals, and we put out coloured matches for those who wished to smoke ... Long cigarette holders became fashionable ... and the ladies, of course, all smoked conscientiously, as the outward and visible sign of sex equality.'

'The feeling, which lasted over several years, was to forget all unpleasant things and to get as much fun out of life as possible. People didn't want to see the social troubles in our midst, and therefore most people ignored these things.'

Charles 'Cockie' Cochran, West End impresario

Non-stop party

There was, wrote Cecil Beaton, 'scarcely a night without some impromptu gathering. Quite often fancy dress taxed one's resourcefulness, but added to the fun'. Beaton's great talent was just then beginning to be noticed, and it gave him an entrée into the charmed circle of BYTs. He recalled that 'Loelia Ponsonby, Zita, Baby and others of the Guinness contingent, organised "stunt" parties, paper chases, find-the-hidden-clue races, bogus impressionist exhibitions and bizarre entertainments based on the fashions of the latest Diaghilev ballets. Loelia, enjoyed devising ingenious ways of eking out her income while living at a spanking pace. She was the first to give parties at which the guests were bidden to make a contribution … providing something high in the gastronomic scale such as oysters, a croute of fois gras, or a bottle of champagne.'

The stunt parties involved such wheezes as storming Selfridges en masse and dancing on the polished counters. Find-the-hidden-clue and paper-chases involved dozens of irresponsible young men haring round the streets of London in sports cars on a mission to acquire objects such as a policeman's helmet or a spider in a matchbox. On one notorious occasion, 300 people received an invitation which read: 'We are having a party with Romps from ten o'clock to bedtime. So write and say you'll come, and we'd love to have Nanny too. Pram park provided. Dress: anything from birth to school age.' Men turned up in rompers or sailor suits, sporting dummies in their mouths. Everyone drank their martinis and manhattans from nursery mugs, and once they were thoroughly tipsy they raced each other through the streets in perambulators. The baby party was denounced as an insult to the innocence of childhood, more shocking somehow than the party that ended with gallons of petrol being poured into the Thames and set alight.

The people who orchestrated such japes had an influence out of all proportion to their numbers or their usefulness. This was partly because many of them were members of ancient aristocratic families, which made them newsworthy, and since the rise of the filmstar was only just beginning, they were the celebrities of their day. Lady Diana Cooper managed to span the divide between the old British nobility and the emerging aristocracy of film and stage by being both a viscountess and an actress. It helped that she was quite fabulously beautiful.

The exclusive attitudes of this elite were expressed in an idiom all their own. Men with beards, those Victorian representatives of all that was old and stuffy, were called 'beavers'. The term was taken up as a taunt by boys and hurled at bearded men in the street. The characteristic Twenties term 'flapper', in its lighthearted modern sense, emanated from these same privileged circles. In earlier generations the word had been a low dialect term for a very young prostitute, a usage that was a metaphorical extension of its original sense: a fledgling duck.

A few years after the radiance of the bright young things had grown altogether dim, Archibald Lyall wrote of the language they used: 'The archetypal upper-class flapper lived, moved and had their hyperbolic being in a world where everything was "quite too thrilling" or "too, too marvellous". And where, instead of being mildly annoyed or amused, one was "purple with rage", "mad with

BELLES OF THE BALL
Society hostesses vied with each other to dream up the most imaginative themes for parties; then their guests had to put together a suitable costume that was simultaneously witty, apt and flattering. Some jolly themes were harder to dress for than others. There were medieval parties, Roman parties, Chinese parties, Mozart parties, the Santa Claus ball, raft parties, mermaid parties – and even 'freak' parties, which posed the particular conundrum of dressing to look ugly in a chic and beautiful way. These young ladies (below), wearing slinky dresses with star-encrusted trains, are off to the Galaxy Ball Pageant at the Park Lane Hotel.

passion", "speechless with laughter", or "quite hysterical", such descriptions being generally reinforced by the most inapposite adverb in the language, "literally".'

Such affected jargon was naturally adopted by outsiders who were neither bright nor young, but wanted to sound as if they were and join the fun. When such people adopted the ways and mannerisms of the smart set, then all the glamour of it somehow began to look rather tawdry and old-hat. Beaton, as a middle-class interloper in this circle, saw it more clearly than most: 'Under Loelia's baton, the Bright Young Things were not only bright but talented. The name, however, when taken up by the gossips, soon acquired a stigma. A "bottle party" became synonymous with drunkenness and squalor, and no longer had any connection with its charter members long before a not very "bright" middle-aged woman shot someone under a piano.' Noël Coward, the wry poet laureate of the Gay Decade, saw it too. His song 'Poor Little Rich Girl', written in 1925, contains the wistful, forward-looking lines:

'In lives of leisure
The craze for pleasure
Steadily grows.
Cocktails and laughter,
But what comes after
Nobody knows …'

PRESENT LAUGHTER
Noël Coward (above, second from left), with theatre producer Charles Cochran, Cochran's wife and three dancers, on board ship from New York to Southampton. Plays such as *Blithe Spirit*, *The Vortex* and *Hay Fever* made Coward rich and famous as a dramatist, but he is perhaps best known as a writer of comic revues and witty romantic songs such as 'Room With A View'. Coward managed to satirise upper class life in the Twenties, while at the same time revelling in it. His works are no mere period pieces, because they say something about the general maladies of 20th-century life – the barely disguised shallowness, the brittle vanity, the aimless pursuit of pleasure. Not that there was anything wrong *per se* in pursuing pleasure: the four ladies in a punt on the Thames during the Henley Regatta (right) seem to be having a perfectly nice, uncomplicated day out.

GET UP AND DANCE

The fact that the brightest young things were from the highest echelons of society made their outrageous escapades, in a de facto way, seem almost acceptable. Or at least, their look and their tastes appeared to those lower down the social scale to be enviable and worthy of imitation. 'This is the Age of Luxury', wrote the *Manchester Guardian* in 1926. 'Before the war and in the uneasy years which immediately followed it, luxury was mainly a matter of means. Now any young typist from Manchester or Kensington can keep her hair trimmed and waved, and her busy feet in fine silk stockings and pale kid shoes.'

The mention of busy feet is a reference to the hypothetical typist's leisure hours, which typically would have been spent dancing. Dance – frenetic, joyful, vivacious dance – was a British obsession in the Twenties. Ethel Mannin, a precocious young novelist and member of the Bohemian fringe, spent many

DINNER DANCE
No sizeable restaurant or hotel could afford to be without a band, a cabaret and a dance floor. Middle-class diners wanted to be serenaded as they ate, and then be able to get up and dance the rest of the night away.

For most of the decade, that constituted the be-all and end-all of a night out – in London, at least, where venues such as the Palm Beach Café on the Thames (left, in 1926) and the Criterion roof garden (above, in 1922) were places to be seen.

evenings dancing at a little nightclub called the Ham Bone in Soho. She also attended 'tea dances and dinner dances and the late-night restaurants with "floor shows" … the Hammersmith Palais de Danse, Prince's in Piccadilly, the Criterion Roof, Romano's in the Strand, the Savoy. It was very smart to dance at the Savoy after the theatre, between the courses of supper.'

There was an ever-changing succession of dances to be mastered – and then discarded like spent matches the moment they became unfashionable. The shimmy, the lindy hop (named in honour of transatlantic aviator Charles Lindbergh), the turkey trot and the camel walk were among those that came and went. The black bottom was another dance fad, which involved stretching out the arms, 'like a man balancing on a tightrope', then making a series of stamping movements while wiggling the hips. If performed poorly the black bottom was distinctly inelegant, which may be one reason it didn't last. Asked to explain both the choreography and the obscure name of the black bottom, one American newsreel commentator suggested that 'the colored kids got the idea from a cow stuck in the mud…'

The American influence

America, of course, was the source of all the new dances flooding into Britain. By far the most popular was the charleston, which was introduced to the country by two exhibition dancers, Robert Sielle and his partner Annette Mills (sister of the actor John Mills and later the presenter of BBC's *Muffin the Mule*). Sielle was American, but the pair were known as the 'English Astaires'. They performed the

OUT ON THE FLOOR

Dancehalls sprang up all over the country during the 1920s, especially once the charleston craze really took off. Some, like The Albert in Glasgow, were Edwardian ballrooms, revamped in a jazzy style for a new and younger clientele. Others, like the Regent Dance Hall in Brighton, were specially built to cash in on the new obsession. When the Regent opened in 1923, a local newspaper described it as 'an artist's expression of exclamation. It is jazz in its highest development. To enter without preparation into that great new hall … is to get the effect of a rocket bursting in one's face … an explosion of all the primary and secondary colours, flung hither and thither in a restless, intersecting criss-cross of blazing light.' Venues varied from the quite small and intimate, like the Parody Club (below), to immense cathedrals dedicated to fun, such as the Hammersmith Palais de Danse (right), where these couples take a breath as they wait for the band to strike up once more.

charleston at the Kit Cat Club in 1925, and from there it spread like an epidemic. The dance was, in essence, a kind of hyped-up hokey-cokey: a frenetic to-and-fro of the legs and arms combined with spectacular set figures that anticipated the jiving craze of the 1950s. The charleston's most eye-catching moves required partners to let go and dance separately. Then they could swing their arms rhythmically in tandem while kicking their legs high or flicking up their heels behind them like frisky, excitable ponies. A dance floor filled with enthusiastic charlestoners was a spectacular sight to behold – and a rather hazardous place to be in the midst of: all bobbing heads and flailing limbs, oscillating rapidly like a mass of pendulums and metronomes in a dizzying, syncopated pattern.

The charleston was wonderfully boisterous and exuberant fun, and that was why people loved it – or else hated it. Office managers complained that employees, in the grip of charleston mania, sat twitching at their desks in an echo of the previous night's revelries, or in anticipation of the next. The *Daily Mail* wrinkled its prim editorial nose and pronounced that the charleston was 'reminiscent only of negro orgies' – even though the dance was actually about as sexually provocative as running on the spot. A vicar in Bristol preached against the charleston from his pulpit, saying 'It is neurotic! It is rotten! It stinks! Phew, open the windows!' But once it became known that the dashing young Prince of Wales enjoyed the charleston – and did it very well, too – then everyone felt that when they danced, they did so by royal appointment.

It was very chic to dance at home to the accompaniment of one's own gramophone. Furniture would be moved to the side of the room, the carpet rolled up and someone would wind up the box so that the music could begin. Imported American recordings were flooding into British music stores, so the latest music was easy to get hold of. The HMV company helpfully produced records with different coloured labels corresponding to genre: red label for classical (not at all the thing for parties) and magenta for light music. A label called Zonophone offered variety and music-hall acts. But it was popular dance music that drove gramophone sales. A quarter of a million machines were produced and sold in 1924; by 1930 that number had reached almost 800,000. Over the same period the number of shellac discs produced annually in Britain went up from 22 million to nearly 72 million. There was no shortage of tunes that you could buy, take home and dance to.

But just as often people went out to a club to dance. In many of these establishments men were supposed to keep their gloves on – which seems a strange point of decorum until one realises that it was a response to the fashion for low-backed dresses and was intended to prevent men touching the bare backs of their dance partners. The West End of London was crammed with louche nightclubs where one could bunny hop to the music of a 'negro band' and drink – illegally – out of hours. And if the place happened to be raided by police, well for the richest and best-connected revellers that was all part of the fun. Many a Bright Young Thing rounded off a night out with an early morning court appearance – followed by a brief encounter, still in evening dress, with the gentlemen of the popular press.

Dancing was a pastime that recognised no social boundaries, and the words of the pre-war Cole Porter hit, 'Everybody's Doing It', sounded almost prophetic:

'Can't you see them all,
Swayin' up the hall,
Let's be gettin' in line,
Everybody's doin' it, doin' it, doin' it ...'

Not everybody had been doing it then, but practically everyone was now. 'Today dancing as an active recreation appeals to many people of all classes', stated the *New Survey of London Life and Labour*, a kind of anthropological study of

> ## 'The hours flew away, I hardly remember whom I danced with – I don't seem to have been very long with anyone ... It was half past four when I got home."
>
> Duff Cooper, diary entry, February 1924

TAPPERS AND KICKERS
In a generation that lived to dance, what could be more glamorous than to be a dancing girl? People enoyed watching dance almost as much as – sometimes more than – doing it themselves, and there was a great vogue for high-kicking chorus girls. The undisputed queens of 'precision dancing' were the Tiller Girls (bottom right), a troupe that had been founded in the last days of the Victorian era, and so had a professional headstart over all the rest. They were masters, so to speak, of the synchronised technique known as 'tap and kick'. They had many imitators, including the cabaret girls of the Piccadilly Hotel, shown here in musically themed frocks (top right). Most people loved a pretty chorus line, but for one cultural commentator, the German sociologist Siegfried Kracauer, the Tiller Girls were not so much dance artists as expressions of the new machine age: 'When they raised their legs with mathematical precision, they joyfully affirmed the progress of rationalisation', he wrote. 'When they continually repeated the same manoeuvre, never breaking ranks, one had the vision of an unbroken chain of automobiles gliding out of the factory.'

continued on page 112

FILM STAR LOOKS

In the comfortable privacy of their own back garden, two thoroughly modern young ladies (right) have fun aspiring to the kind of glamour that they could only have picked up from the movies. The parasol and bathing costumes epitomise the right kind of look. The portable gramophone was an essential adjunct to any kind of a good time, while the ukelele – an icon of the Jazz Age – was enjoying its first flush of popularity with amateur players.

The actress Joan Barry (below) had a brief but distinguished film career in the 1920s, spanning the switchover from silent movies to talkies. She made the switch in a rather unusual way, when she was hired by Alfred Hitchcock to dub the voice of the Czech actress Anny Ondra in his 1929 thriller *Blackmail*. When the film went into production it was intended to be silent, so the fact that Ondra had an East European accent did not matter. But by the time the film was finished, talkies were all the rage, so *Blackmail* was reworked with sound. Barry received no credit for her voiceover, but she did go on to star in a later Hitchcock movie, *Rich and Strange*. Her look was more sophisticated than this picture of her suggests.

working-class tribes in the capital, written in 1928. 'The dance-halls are within the range of nearly everybody's purse, and typists, shop assistants and factory girls rub shoulders in them. People drop into a palais after work or on Saturday evenings as casually as they go to a cinema.' The dance-hall owners were of course delighted that their venues were filled to the brim. 'The younger generation of the British people have come to love the jazz step, as it typifies pep, energy, push, advancement, the love of living, and the things that go with an up-to-date modern world', wrote an anonymous contributor to the monthly *Hammersmith Palais Dancing News*.

In the north of England, where dancing was called 'jigging', the nightly ritual of the dance halls had a complex social etiquette all of its own. Inside the great barn-like interiors, young men would gather in the half-light on one side of the hall, while the women arraigned themselves like rows of trinkets in a jeweller's shop window on the other. One by one the men would cross the floor and choose a partner. The girls left standing – and there were usually plenty of them – would resignedly dance with each other, hoping that their moves, if not their looks, would catch the attention of a male dancing partner. In many such dance halls, the

STARS OF THE STAGE
Jessie Matthews (above) had success in the Twenties as a comedy actress, taking the lead in several of Noël Coward's revues. The details of her private life were minutely recorded in the newspapers and her career suffered during the divorce trial of her lover (her future husband). Matthews recovered from the scandal to become one of the most popular British stars of the 1930s.

More highbrow entertainment was provided by ballet. These two dancers (right), in knitted costumes designed by Coco Chanel, are performing a modernist piece called 'Le Train Bleu'. Although born Hilda Munnings and Sydney Healey-Kay, as dancers they became Lydia Sokolova and Anton Dolin – Russian-sounding stage-names were de rigueur in the days of Diaghilev's Ballet Russes.

DANCING FOR HEALTH

The dance craze was often criticised for being damaging to the health and morals of British youth, but not all the nation's dancing was done in dim, smoke-filled halls. There were some idealistic innovators trying to show that dance, properly interpreted, was a wholesome, elevating activity. One of the leading proponents of this idea was Margaret Morris. She was deeply influenced by the modernist dancer Isadora Duncan, and from Duncan's brother she had learned a set of movements which, he believed, were an authentic reflection of the dance of the ancient Greeks. Morris adapted these movements and built them into a system of artistic gymnastics and therapeutic choreography (seen in action, above). She had some small success in interesting the medical establishment in her method, and sowed the idea – still current – that dance can be a useful form of physiotherapy and physical exercise.

proceedings were overseen by a master of ceremonies, who was something of a cross between a headmaster and a chaperone. 'Our major domo stood five feet one – a pocket Valentino in evening dress', wrote Robert Roberts, who grew up in Salford between the wars. 'He had a fearsome reputation as a Don Juan and was alleged to have fathered no fewer than seven bastards on the hall's lady patrons. In his way our MC was a stickler for decorum. He came down heavily on any males gyrating as they smoked, or with their hats on. That, he felt, lowered the tone.'

THE FLICKS AND TALKIES

The other main entertainment that drew the masses was the flickering silver screen. In the darkness of the picture house, ordinary people entered another world inhabited by silent smouldering 'vamps' like Theda Bara. The studio promotional material claimed that she had been born in Egypt and that her name was two anagrams: Theda was death rearranged (terribly daring) and Bara was the reverse of Arab, a byword for the exotic. In fact, she was the daughter of a Jewish tailor

continued on page 120

PICTURE PALACES

The Tooting Electric Pavilion was a typical old-style cinema, built in 1914 when film was still in its infancy. By the mid-1920s it was rather run-down, its appearance not helped by the line of washing, which some bright spark had decided was a good way to promote the Mary Pickford film *Suds*. As films became more sophisticated, so too did the buildings in which they were shown. The next generation of cinemas was more like the New Gallery, Regent Street, which in the mid-1920s was given a brightly illuminated canopy – and a uniformed doorman to add a note of exclusivity. Inside was a spectacular, 256-foot long Greek frieze and one of London's finest Wurlitzers. In the 1930s, the New Gallery became well-known as the theatre in which Disney's feature cartoons were premiered. The Tooting Electric also went up in the world: its façade was remodelled in Art Deco style in 1933 and it was renamed the Astoria. It was demolished in the 1970s, but the interior of the New Gallery still survives.

FILM STARS

It was in the 1920s that movie stars became household names. Charlie Chaplin had blazed the trail – he was famous before the Great War – but in the 1920s cinema-goers began to feel somehow personally acquainted with the people up on the screen. They could see them up close, by the end of the decade they could hear their voices, and through the gossip columns and fan magazines they gained a delicious peek at their private lives.

KINGS OF COMEDY
Both Stan Laurel and Oliver Hardy – seen here (left) taking a break from filming *The Finishing Touch* – served a long comic apprenticeship. Laurel (on the right) was born in Ulverston, Lancashire. He worked in music hall and was understudy to Charlie Chaplin before emigrating to the USA in 1912. Hardy was a singer who became a silent film performer. He made more than 250 films before pairing up with Laurel in their hugely successful double act in the mid-20s. But for many movie-goers, Buster Keaton was the finest visual comedian of them all. Despite his mournful face – seen below in *Sherlock Junior* made in 1928 – he was less mawkish, more inventive and in the end simply funnier than Chaplin.

TICKET OFFICE

Adults 40¢

Adults 40¢

Childern 10¢

DIVANS 50¢

HOW MANY

BEHIND THE MASKS

Charlie Chaplin, seen here in 1929 (left), contemplating a mannequin of his on-screen persona. Chaplin was the first global superstar, his worldwide fame made possible by the universal language of silent film. The 1920s were the first decade of international celebrity. Theda Bara (above) made a name for herself with a darkly sexy persona that was every bit as manufactured and fictional as Chaplin's little hobo. Ronald Colman (above right) was the genuine article: a handsome veteran of the Western Front who did his own stunts despite a serious war wound to his leg. In the silent era Colman was often

paired with the Hungarian actress Vilma Banky; they are seen here in a publicity shot for *Night of Love*. Romance was a staple of silent cinema, and no-one did wordless passion better than Greta Garbo. In *The Temptress* (bottom right), she was paired with Antonio Moreno, but she smouldered best in the embrace of John Gilbert – 'the great lover' – with whom she had a very public affair.

Chaplin, Colman and Garbo all survived the transition to dialogue-led movies, heralded in 1927 by Al Jolson's groundbreaking talkie *The Jazz Singer* (centre right). Theda Bara, already past her prime, faded away in the middle of the decade.

'A tramp, a gentleman, a poet, a dreamer, a lonely fellow, always hopeful of romance and adventure.'

Charlie Chaplin, describing his down-at-heel on-screen alter ego

PULLING OUT ALL THE STOPS
The organ at the Davis cinema in Croydon.
Organ music was an integral part of the
entertainment on a night out at the flicks.
In the first part of the decade, the function
of the organ was to provide a musical
soundtrack to the silent film on screen.
Often it was down to the organist to
improvise mood music as he went along.
Once talkies became popular, the
musician's job changed. He would play for
half an hour before the film to 'warm up'
the audience, then again during the
intermission when the performance often
turned into a communal sing-song. Finally,
at the end of the programme, the audience
would stand for the national anthem, and
the organist would then continue to play as
they left the building. Some of the organs
were magnificently engineered instruments,
rendered all the more spectacular if they
were mounted on a mechanical lift, so as to
rise magically from the orchestra pit at the
start of each performance, sinking back
down as the last notes played.

from Poland and Theda was her childhood nickname, shortened from her real name, Theodosia, while Bara came from her maternal grandfather's name, Baranger. The audiences for films such as Bara's *Unchastened Woman* consisted overwhelmingly of young wage-earners with money to spare. Young working girls, in particular, spent their money on going to the pictures two or three times a week. Well into the Thirties, there were cheap 'flea-pits' that charged just a penny a ticket to watch a film. Up-market picture houses were a more expensive outing, but a fellow could easily treat his girl to the cinema for less than couple of shillings and – if she was agreeable – spend a couple of cosy hours entwined on the double seats that many establishments provided at the back of the auditorium.

Disapproving voices

Some moral policemen objected to the cinema on precisely these grounds – that they provided a place out of the home for courtship – and so did some actual policemen. The chief constable of Guildford felt constrained to point out that picture houses were places 'where young men and women attend together not for the purpose of following the pictures, but to be spoony', as if 'spooniness' were an arrestable offence. Another attempt to link the flicks to crime – and one which has had echoes through the years since – was made by Lilian Russell, wife of Charles Russell, the Chief Inspector of Reformatory and Industrial Schools before the war. 'The cinema-play, though not exactly vicious, is often very low in tone, giving young people who frequent it an altogether false and vulgar, foolishly sentimental, and in the worst sense, Americanised view of life … We have seen not a few weak-willed young fellows in prison who have been convicted for thefts committed, as they confessed, to get money to "buy some tabs [cigarettes] and go to the pictures".' Russell spent the Twenties trying to drag teenagers out of the flea-pits and into the wholesome embrace of the Lads' Clubs over which she presided.

The content of the 'cinema-plays' against which Mrs Russell fulminated was in any case not nearly so deleterious as she believed. The British Board of Film Censors made sure of that by enforcing a long list of banned scenes and subjects. Among the items on the banned list are: 'the modus operandi of criminals … indecorous dancing … scenes in which the king and officers in uniform are seem in an odious light … "first night" scenes … vitriol throwing … women fighting with knives … salacious wit … drunken scenes carried to excess … surgical operations … outrageous and irreverent sub-titles … commitment of crime by children … criminal poisoning by the dissemination of germs … realistic horrors of war.' Yet while many of the interdictions are laughable or unfathomable, one or two, such as the prohibition of 'insistence on the inferiority of coloured races' are laudable and were ahead of their time.

'It is not the single talkie drama that does the harm, but the cumulative effect of many which affect the impressionable mind as a stone is worn by the dropping of water.'

Lilian Russell, determined critic of the social effects of the cinema

The coming of talkies

But the magical allure of the cinema was barely affected by the carping of its detractors. In fact, the magnetic draw of the silver screen grew stronger year by year. For one thing, the venues themselves grew more attractive as out-dated Edwardian cinemas were replaced and reinvented as splendid 'picture palaces' in the form of Egyptian temples, Roman villas and Moorish citadels. Art Deco was a very popular style as cinemas became spectacular places to visit. But more important than any transformation of the venue, in 1928 the nature of the spectacle itself changed when talkies burst onto the screen. The first talkie was *The Jazz Singer*, starring Al Jolson; the first spoken sentence in film history consisted of four words captured by accident as he was about to break into song. They were, appropriately enough, 'Ma, listen to this'.

That summons spelled the end for the silent movie, but not everyone realised it at first. Though talkies were a technological step forward, they were for some reason viewed by highbrow commentators – the kind of people who said *k*inema rather than *s*inema – as an inferior art form compared to silent film. The *New Statesman* denigrated talkies in general as 'squawkies'; one journalist writing in the normally demotic *Sunday Express* declared, with massive hyperbole and no feeling for popular opinion, that 'the voice of feminine Hollywood is a pentecostal calamity'. Even *Punch*, usually good-humoured and good at spotting a trend, said in its review of *The Jazz Singer* that 'the silent film is not seriously threatened'.

The following year the same magazine vilified cinema audiences generally. 'The film public is a doped public', wrote *Punch*. 'They sit in a stupor, hypnotised by the organ and the comfy seats and the legs of the blonde, incapable of criticism and swallowing without protest things which, if they saw them in the theatre, would cause them to rise up, boo, and go out.' But the cinema-going public didn't care two hoots for the snobbish opinions of journalists. In 1930 the silent-versus-talkie debate was settled once and for all by a new film, *The Kiss*, starring Greta

Garbo. It was advertised with huge posters reading simply 'GARBO TALKS'. People flocked to the picture palaces to hear the husky, sexy tones of the Swedish ice-maiden: 'Gimme a visky, ginger ale on the side. And don't be stinchy, baby ...'

OPENING UP THE AIRWAVES

The rise of cinema was not the only media revolution of the Twenties. At the start of the decade, 'wireless telephony' was still a rather dull technical hobby, pursued by the kind of man who stayed at home in the evenings and smoked a pipe. It was about to transform the way that people amused and informed themselves.

All wireless users in Britain were required to apply to the Postmaster General for a licence. This document gave the holder permission for 'the installation and use of a station for receiving wireless signals for experimental purposes'. The crystal receivers came in kit form and had to be assembled before use. There were no programmes broadcast at all, so the sport, such as it was, consisted entirely in seeing if one could pick up a signal. Hobbyists would don their headphones and tune in to an engineer of the Marconi Company who, ensconced in Chelmsford, might recite nursery rhymes or lists of railway stations. The keenest enthusiasts would attempt to pick up signals from further afield – Paris, Luxembourg, Berlin.

The wireless habit, in effect, was a bit like aural angling, fishing for distant signals. When the Prince of Wales visited Mill Hill School in the early Twenties he congratulated the boys on having managed to 'wireless the Atlantic' and pick up a signal from America. But to most people the whole business was quite baffling. In 1923, when the wireless was demonstrated to the Archbishop of Canterbury, he asked if he ought not open the window to let the signal in.

RIDING THE CREST OF THE WAVES
Wireless technology developed in tandem with the programme content. As the decade progressed, receivers became simpler to operate and began to look less like the contents of an electrician's workshop, more like polished mahogany vanity cases. At the same time, the transmission of popular light music became the main function of the new devices. These serious fellows, photographed in 1922 (above), are unwittingly on the very cusp of that transformation, as they link their valve radios in series in order to channel a musical programme through a loudspeaker.

Back in Chelmsford, the Marconi engineers had long since grown bored of chanting nonsense into a microphone, and in 1920 invited two local singers – a Mrs Winifred Sayer and a Mr Edward Cooper, a tenor with a day job in Marconi's factory – to sing a few pieces on their 'experimental' wavelength. These two amateurs thus became the first artistes ever to showcase their talents to the British people. From that small beginning grew the immense social phenomenon of wireless broadcasting. Later the same year, Dame Nellie Melba was persuaded to go to Chelmsford to give a recital which, it was said incredulously, could be heard 'within a radius of a thousand miles'.

Birth of the BBC
At this stage the potential audience was still tiny, so the Marconi Company decided to discontinue its broadcasts. But the protests of the small band of experimenters were so voluble that the largest manufacturers of crystal sets became convinced they would be able to sell large numbers – if only there were interesting broadcasts to be received. So in 1922 they set up a private concern called the British Broadcasting Company Ltd to make programmes for the wireless.

Their speculative venture was a huge and unexpected success. The opportunity to have entertainment piped straight into one's home – all of it as healthful and wholesome as the water that came out of the scullery tap – was something people were prepared to pay for. At the time, it was still only possible to listen in on headphones, but that did not seem to matter. Music dominated the BBC's early broadcasts: dance band music, of course, played by the likes of Jack Payne and the Hotel Cecil Orchestra, but also light orchestral pieces, brass ensembles and classical music. Few people were put off by the high proportion of highbrow broadcasts. (*Punch* ran a cartoon showing a man listening in with a rather pained expression on his face as his wife asks 'What is it, dear? Bad news or Stravinsky?') The provision of enjoyable content was to transform the wireless from a rather dull potting-shed pastime into the single most powerful mass medium in the country. In the four years after the BBC was incorporated, the number of wireless licensees rose from 6,000 to 2 million, reaching 9 million by 1939, and the cartel of wireless manufacturers was growing rich from the sales of their equipment.

The monopoly of the airwaves was, in the opinion of the government, too precious to remain in private hands. So in 1927, during the Conservative administration of Stanley Baldwin, the shareholders of the British Broadcasting Company were bought out with state funds and the organisation, with all its staff and infrastructure, was nationalised. To reflect the change in its status, the Company was renamed the British Broadcasting Corporation, a formula which neatly preserved the three initials by which it was already known. The new BBC's main broadcasting station was moved to Borough Hill near Daventry in Northamptonshire, a conveniently high and geographically central point from which to broadcast to the entire island. 'Daventry calling …' would later become the verbal signature of the BBC Empire Service, recognised and revered by Anglophiles and British expats around the globe.

MUSIC TO THE EAR
Right from the start, the mission of the BBC was to 'educate, inform and entertain', but most of the audience were far more interested in entertainment than anything else. Music, above all, was the thing that got people listening to the wireless. It seemed little short of miraculous that one could sit at home and listen to an orchestra that was playing miles away. The novelty of the experience was expressed in the name the 'Invisible Band' (below), photographed performing at the BBC's Savoy Hill Studio, off the Strand in London, in December 1923. Broadcasts that came under the 'educate' category were not such crowd-pleasers. It is hard to imagine that many tuned in to listen when Mr Robert Lindsay (top right) of the British Dental Association delivered his lecture on the state of the nation's teeth.

LISTEN WITH PALMER

Much of the BBC's output in the early years was created on the hoof. The smartly dressed gentleman in spats and bow tie is Rex Palmer (right), a veteran of the Royal Flying Corps and one of the founders of the Corporation. He was known to thousands of children as 'Uncle Rex', as he was one of the BBC staffers who took it upon themselves to display their talents in *Children's Hour*, a 'nightly romp' filled with childish misbehaviour. 'Uncle-ing' became a kind of semi-professional hobby for Palmer and several other BBC executives, who received sacks of fan mail from children. Palmer also happened to be a fine baritone and sang 'Abide With Me' to the nation at the close of programmes every Sunday.

MZX CALLING
'This is the Marconi valve transmitter at Chelmsford, England, testing on a wavelength of 2,800 metres ... I will now recite for you my usual collection of British railway stations for test purposes ...'
That was about as exciting as the wireless got at the start of the 1920s. To liven things up a bit – and also 'for test purposes' – enthusiasts experimented with different ways and means of picking up the signal. People naturally tried to catch radio waves while in their motorcars – though this involved stopping by the roadside and laboriously setting up the aerial and other apparatus. This early enthusiast has attached the wiring to his pipe, to pick up a signal outdoors while enjoying a smoke.

The impact on British life of the creation of the BBC is hard to underestimate. It allowed the wireless to develop as a public service, independent of commercial or political pressures. The Corporation, under the terms of its Royal Charter, did not belong to government. If it belonged to anyone, that person was John Reith, the general manager of the organisation. Reith was deeply committed to the BBC's mission to 'educate, inform and entertain', a formula which he himself devised. And he never allowed the politicians to use the organisation as a megaphone or a mouthpiece, not even in times of crisis such as the General Strike of 1926 – in fact, especially at such times. National leaders, when they spoke on the wireless, were merely borrowing the airwaves to put their case to the nation. The listening public, for their part, formed judgments based on the speakers' voices, arguments and conviction. It added up to a unique and democratic use of the new technology. The wireless raised people's social and political awareness, it functioned as a source of new knowledge and ideas, it spoke across and above social barriers, and so worked as a positive force for change in an already rapidly changing world.

WORKING ON THE BOX

In the middle of the decade, as wireless sets were becoming a fixture in every home, a Scottish engineer named John Logie Baird – right and below, with fellow-Scot and actor Jack Buchanan (seated) – was working on transmitting moving pictures. The story goes that in 1925, in an upstairs lab in Soho, he succeeded in broadcasting the image of a ventriloquist's dummy's head from his transmitter to a receiver in the next room. Soon after he did the same with a live head, that of an office boy called William Taynton, who thus went down in history as the first person ever seen on the screen of a 'televisor', as Baird called his set. In 1929, Baird persuaded the BBC to take an interest in his invention. But his system depended on mechanical revolving discs inside both the transmitter and receiver – as seen in his stripped-down prototype (right) – and this turned out to be a technological dead end. The form of television that eventually caught on exploited an entirely different principle, based on the cathode ray tube.

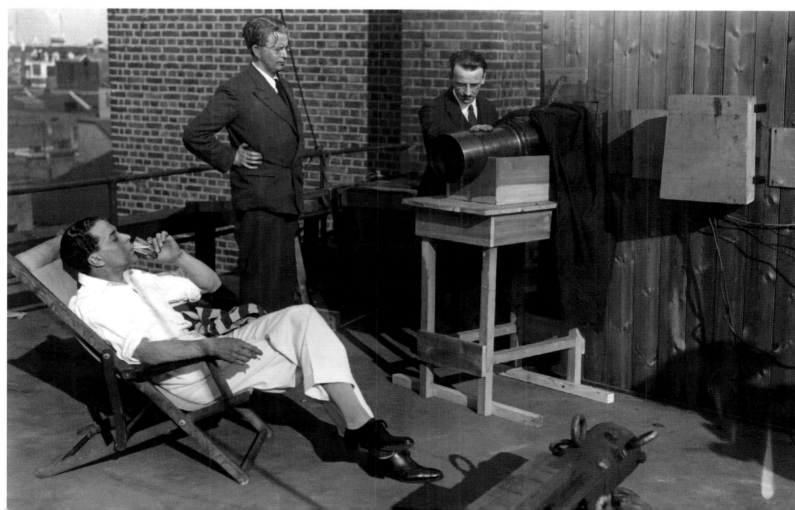

SUNNY SIDE
OF THE STREET?

Most working people in Britain felt insecure in their jobs as the Twenties wore on, but possibly no-one more so than the Prime Minister. Running the country was a precarious business – the occupant of 10 Downing Street changed no fewer than six times over the course of the decade. From 1923 the same two figures kept coming round and round, like the wooden toys on a Swiss clock. The post-war premier, David Lloyd George, was succeeded in 1922 by Andrew Bonar Law, who was followed by Stanley Baldwin in 1923, Ramsay MacDonald in January 1924, then Baldwin again later that same year. MacDonald was back in 1929 to preside over government until 1935, when he was ousted once more by Baldwin.

HORSE AND GROOM Workmen cleaning the Quadriga on top of the Wellington Arch, high above Hyde Park Corner, in an era when attitudes to 'health and safety' were very different from today.

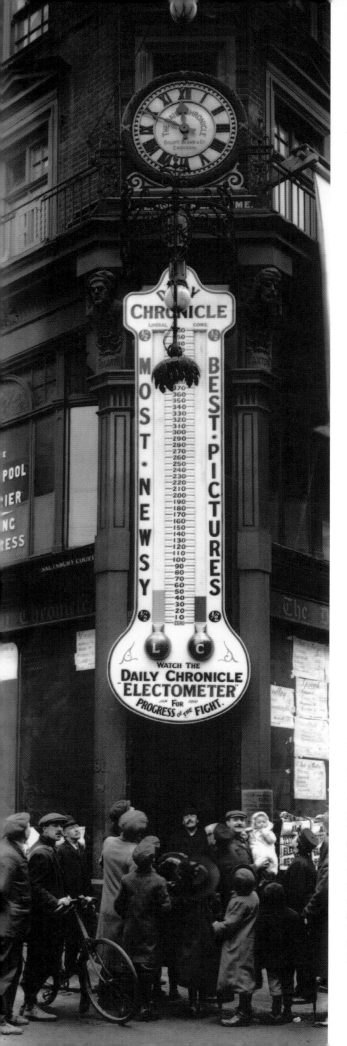

MINISTERS OF THE CROWN

Broadly speaking, the frequent changes of leadership were one symptom of the economic sickness that was rapidly spreading through the land, but in the case of Andrew Bonar Law it was a personal illness that made his time as Prime Minister so short. Soon after taking office he was diagnosed with throat cancer. He resigned both as PM and as Conservative Party leader in May 1923, by which time the condition had made it impossible for him to speak in Parliament. His tenure was 209 days in all, which was too little time to make much of a mark, other than giving him the distinction of being the shortest-serving Prime Minister in British history. He died six months after leaving office. At his funeral in Westminster Abbey, Lord Asquith remarked that they were burying the Unknown Prime Minister next to the Unknown Soldier. The jibe became Bonar Law's unofficial epitaph – unfairly, because he had a long and distinguished career in Parliament and public life before he became PM. It was cruel, too, because Bonar Law had lost two sons in the War. For all anyone knew, the unknown prime minister was being laid to rest beside one of his own boys.

The mantle of leadership was picked up by Bonar Law's chancellor, Stanley Baldwin. Baldwin saw himself as the pipe-smoking kindly uncle of the people, an image that he projected rather well. He used the new-fangled wireless to speak directly to the public, and his broadcasts often took the form of self-deprecating fireside chats. But if the medium and the method were novel, the message was noble and old-fashioned. 'I am just one of yourselves, who has been called to special work for the country at this time', he told the public when he first became Prime Minister. 'I never sought the office. I never planned out or schemed my life. I have but one idea, which was an idea that I inherited … service to the people of this country. All my life I believed from my heart the words of Browning: "All service ranks the same with God". It makes very little difference whether a man is

HOT NEWS
A Fleet Street newspaper trials the 'electometer' – a novel way to bring the public up-to-the minute news about election results. Britain's political climate changed radically in the 1920s. The Liberal Party, a major force in politics for generations, went into rapid decline. The Labour Party enjoyed a corresponding rise and the prevalence of socialist ideas created a new ideological environment in the country. The Conservative Party had to find strategies to deal with the changed conditions – and with a different primary opponent. Much of the civil strife in the 1920s was a struggle between the reds and the blues, between the aggrieved working classes on the one hand and the stout bourgeoisie on the other.

CONSERVATIVE LEADERS

Andrew Bonar Law, photographed while inspecting a troop of boys at Kew in southwest London (right), is little remembered as Prime Minister today, partly because he did not have time to prove himself in office, but also because in the course of his career he was often outshone by more ebullient personalities, such as David Lloyd George. And he was modest about his own political gifts; he is said to have remarked of Asquith that 'he can make a better speech drunk than the rest of us can sober'. Bonar Law's resignation through illness opened the way for his successor Stanley Baldwin (below). Baldwin's manner was self-confident, his style might now be termed 'presidential'. A born delegator, he left ministries to look after themselves. He did the minimum of paperwork, preferring to issue orders and make his views known through speaking personally to the right individual. He drank champagne to 'buoy himself up', and left the office promptly at 5pm on a Friday.

'Generation after generation will come, and the spear of justice will still be in the hands of good and upright men and women … I see no end, thank God, to these things.'

Ramsay MacDonald, looking to the future after becoming the first Labour Prime Minister in 1924

driving a tramcar or sweeping streets or being prime minister, if he only brings to that service everything that is in him and performs it for the sake of mankind.'

Baldwin's solution for the nation's economic troubles was, in one word, protectionism. He proposed to safeguard British jobs and British products by placing a high tax on foreign goods, with only a slightly lower one on imports from the Empire. Big business was delighted, but most people were appalled by the prospect of paying more for their food. The policy was particularly unpopular with the recently enfranchised female section of the electorate, since they were generally the ones charged with managing the household budget. For the amusement of worried British shoppers, a newspaper published a new set of words to the popular song 'Yes, We Have No Bananas'. The rewritten lyric ran:

'No, we won't have Protection,
We won't have Protection today.
'Twould rush up the prices,
And squeeze us like vices.
And we'd have to pay, pay, pay …'

Baldwin called a general election in order to get the people's mandate for his high-tariff policy – but he did not get the result he wanted. The outcome was a hung parliament, in which the Conservatives won 258 seats, the Liberals 159 and the Labour Party – suddenly a political force to be reckoned with – won 191. The Liberal Party declined to support the Conservatives, so in January 1924 the government resigned. King George V then called on the Labour leader, Ramsay MacDonald, to form a government. 'They have different ideas to ours as they are all socialists', he confided to his royal diary. 'But they ought to be given a chance and treated fairly.' MacDonald accepted the King's call and the first Labour government in British history came into being.

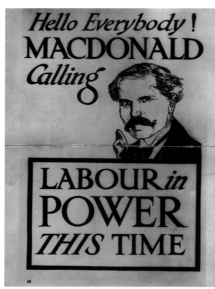

THE POWER AND THE GLORY
It was an historic moment when Ramsay MacDonald (above, standing) became the first Labour Prime Minister in January 1924. He led a minority government, so it is no surprise that his tenure turned out to be shortlived, lasting only 10 months. When he called another election in October 1924, MacDonald asked the British people to give him the executive might of a Prime Minister, in addition to the mere job title. But for the time being the public remained unconvinced by the socialist experiment – and power passed back to the Tories.

LABOUR IN POWER

The prospect of MacDonald and his newly appointed proletarian ministers going to the palace to be sworn in gave rise to much snobbish tittering. Would these horny-handed sons of toil know how to wear court dress, and would they even agree to do so? Would their rough manners let them down? In the event nothing untoward happened, but the day that Labour took office was no less remarkable for that. Among the men who swore the ministerial oath was John Robert Clynes, who began his working life in a Lancashire cotton mill at the age of ten, and was now chairman of the parliamentary party. 'I could not help marvelling at the strange turn of Fortune's wheel', he later wrote, 'which had bought Ramsay MacDonald the starving clerk, J H Thomas the engine driver, Arthur Henderson the foundry labourer and Clynes the mill-hand to this pinnacle beside the man

whose forebears had been kings for so many splendid generations.' From his own exalted perspective, George V was thinking along similar lines: 'Today 23 years ago dear Grandmama died. I wonder what she would have thought of a Labour Government!' Grandmama – that is, Queen Victoria – would probably have thought that the political landscape had been turned upside down. It had certainly been changed for ever.

With less than 200 MPs out of nearly 700, the first Labour government faced an impossible task. Nevertheless, it forced through some commendable measures to help the poorest citizens, the ones who had been hit hardest by the slump. Unemployment benefit, for example, was raised from 15 shillings to 18 shillings a week. If a man had a dependent wife, then he received 7 shillings on top, and he was entitled to claim 2 shillings a week for each child. So an unemployed man who was married with three children received benefit amounting to 31 shillings a week in the summer of 1924. It was still not enough to live on – a government

continued on page 139

SOUP AND SOCIALISM
The shortlived Labour government did what it could for the poor and unemployed. At the most basic level, this meant providing hot meals at 'poor relief' soup kitchens. Some of those out of work had unemployment insurance, but a government committee appointed by the incoming Conservative administration found that public opinion was 'predominantly unfavourable' to any form of dole because it was thought to encourage idleness. The committee investigated the widespread assumption that the unemployed routinely abused the insurance system, but found no evidence of fraud at all.

END OF THE LINE

The hulk of HMS *Lion* blends with its own dark reflection to make almost a perfect circle on the still water of a dock in Jarrow on the River Tyne. The fate of this distinguished ship mirrored the experience of many a British serviceman. The *Lion* had performed valiant service in the Great War. She took part in the Battle of Heligoland Bight in the first days of the conflict, and assisted in the sinking of the German cruiser SMS *Köln*. She survived 18 hits at the Battle of Dogger Bank in 1915, where she served as Admiral Beatty's flagship. In May 1916, on the eve of the Battle of the Somme, she took part in the Battle of Jutland. For her crew, this was their own seaborne Somme: 99 seamen and marines were killed on board. Among them was Major Francis Harvey who, though mortally wounded, took measures to prevent fire reaching the ship's ammunition store. He ordered the magazine doors closed and the magazine flooded. His action – and that of the gunnery crew who carried out the order – saved the ship and the lives of many other crew members. Harvey was posthumously awarded the Victoria Cross.

In the post-war world, HMS *Lion* was surplus to naval requirements. In 1924 she was sold for scrap and taken to Jarrow to be stripped. It was here, against a backdrop of smoke and heavy industry, that she was photographed in her sadly diminished state. Soon after this picture was taken, what was left of the *Lion* was towed to Scotland, where she was finally broken up.

statistician had calculated that a working docker with a wife and three children required a minimum income of £3 13s 6d a week. But under previous administrations, there had been nothing at all for a wife or children, so the unemployed under Labour were already much better off than they had been under either the Liberals or the Tories.

Making an impact in housing

The Labour government's other great undertaking for the benefit of the poor working classes was the 1924 Housing Act. This new law empowered local authorities to build houses for low-paid citizens – something that no private speculators were doing at the time. 'Are we to remain without houses merely because people with money to invest refuse to invest that money directly in working-class houses?' asked John Wheatley, the main sponsor of the Act, a fiery left-wing Glaswegian whom MacDonald had appointed Minister of Health. The answer to Wheatley's question was a resounding no: a Labour government had a responsibility to house the ordinary people who were the engine of the nation's prosperity, or at least of its recovery.

The health and well-being of the people who would live in the new houses was paramount. Wheatley houses were built twelve to an acre on the outskirts of big towns. This relatively low density allowed light and air to surround every home and gave each occupier a patch of garden in which to grow vegetables. It was also written into the Bill that all the houses must have an indoor bathroom (rather than provision for a copper in the scullery). Altogether more than half a million municipal homes were eventually constructed under the auspices of Wheatley's Act, and building homes for ordinary people became one of the primary functions of local councils. In retrospect, this was the main legacy of that first Labour government – a solid, unquestionably sound, bricks-and-mortar achievement.

The Tories return to power

The successes of MacDonald's first administration are all the more remarkable when one considers that it lasted less than a year. In 1925, the baton passed back to the Conservatives under Stanley Baldwin. With Churchill as Chancellor, one of the first acts of the administration was to return the pound to the gold standard, which had been suspended on the outbreak of war in 1914. Reinstatement was intended to restore British prestige and return the economy to its 'normal' pre-war level, but the pound had fallen in real terms, so it merely made British exports artificially expensive in foreign markets. The economy suffered as a result.

An even more dangerous economic crisis was looming in the mining industry. Colliery owners had seen their profits fall, and wanted to cut miners' wages. The miners refused to countenance this, claiming that they were already worse off than they had been in 1914. In April 1926, the owners posted notices saying that employees would be locked out – sacked, in other words – unless they agreed to a much lower wage and a longer working day. It was a move designed to provoke a showdown and the miners took up the challenge. They turned to the union movement to support them, arguing that if the miners were forced to take pay cuts, then other workers would also be forced down the same route. The TUC agreed and declared a general strike for the first week of May.

THE GENERAL STRIKE

Once again, revolution seemed to be in the air. While the unions finalised their plans to paralyse the country, the government made preparations to foil them. Hyde Park was turned into a vast depot for food and other essential supplies. Three thousand lorries were parked up there, with military guards posted on the gates, and loyal Post Office workers worked through the night stringing telephone wires between the blossoming trees. On the eve of the strike, *The Times* wrote portentously that 'unless counsels of reason prevail, we are within a few hours of the gravest domestic menace which has hung over this nation since the fall of the

THE STRIKERS

Though the striking workers saw themselves as active participants in a fundamental struggle, for many there was little they could actually do to fill the days. These Scottish miners from Prestonpans colliery in East Lothian (above) could find nothing better to do than sit and play cards, while the political drama played itself out elsewhere. In Plymouth, this orderly column of men (left) are marching not to the barricades, but to a church pew. Dressed in their Sunday best, they are about to attend a special service for strikers at St Andrew's church. Not all clergy were so sympathetic. That same Sunday, 9 May, the Roman Catholic Archbishop of Westminster declared that the strike was 'a sin against God'. Information about what was going on was hard to come by, and so was consumed avidly by strikers when it appeared (right). Local branches of the TUC and other left-wing organisations produced newsheets with names such as *The Worker*, but there were precious few means of getting them distributed to supporters. Strikers in the provinces relied on an almost medieval system of TUC 'couriers', who travelled from city to city spreading news by word of mouth and encouraging men to stand firm.

Stuarts'. And as in the days that led up to the English Civil War, there was a grand taking of sides. It was almost impossible to be neutral: everyone was either for the strike or adamantly against it.

The middle classes were almost uniformly against. When the government called for people to take the strikers' places, the white-collared office workers and small businessmen were the first to volunteer to 'do their bit' – as if driving a tram, manning a signal box, or lugging sides of beef were a patriotic duty on a par with fighting the Germans in the war. The ranks of the pro-government men were swelled by students from Oxford and Cambridge, who viewed the strike was an attack on ancient British liberties and responded enthusiastically to the government's call. On the morning of 3 May, great crowds of them could be seen in the quad of the Foreign Office, smoking and laughing and waiting to be given a job to do: most of them were enrolled as special constables.

ARMED GUARDS
Armoured cars – of a type cruelly familiar to the people of Ireland – were used to protect convoys of food during the General Strike (above). In London military muscle was on display throughout the crisis. A pair of destroyers was moored in the Pool of London, where warehouses were full of supplies, and a battalion was stationed close to the docks in Victoria Park – they shared the space with crowds attending pro-strike rallies. As far as the strikers were concerned, armoured cars were deployed for propaganda purposes, as the TUC had pledged not to interfere with the distribution of food or medical supplies.

READY FOR A FIGHT
Students from Oxford University (top right) pose with their standard-issue tin hats, armbands and wooden truncheons after being enrolled as special constables. On 5 May, at the height of the strike, the government announced that it intended to recruit 50,000 specials in London, and to mobilise 200,000 second-reserve policemen throughout the country. Some received training in combat techniques. By this time, the government had nearly half a million volunteers at its disposal. Most were involved in more peaceable anti-strike work, such as distributing the petrol stockpiled in Hyde Park (right).

DISPLAYING THEIR COLOURS
Not all working-class people were in favour of the strike. These fishermen's wives from Cullercoats, just north of Tynemouth, have dressed in their traditional shawls in order to demonstrate against it. Most of the other workers in the industrial Northeast – above all the miners – were solidly behind the action. Some strike supporters even resorted to sabotage. On Monday 10 May, the Flying Scotsman, which was being driven by volunteers, was derailed close to Newcastle and it was discovered that a section of track had been deliberately removed. Fortunately, of the 500 passengers on board, only one was hurt.

The strike began in earnest that night when the 'first-line workers' downed tools, among them railwaymen, printers, builders, steelworkers, stokers and labourers in power stations. As it turned out, the decision to bring the printers out was the first tactical error by the unions, as they found it hard to get their views across while the strike was on. The government, meanwhile, produced a newssheet called *The British Gazette*, the combative tone of which was entirely due to the character of its editor, Winston Churchill. On 7 May, the *Gazette* reported the view of Liberal MP Sir John Simon that the strike was 'an utterly illegal proceeding' since it was aimed at the government and not at the employers.

Churchill tried to extend the reach of his propaganda by commandeering the airwaves, but was stoutly resisted by the BBC general manager John Reith ('that wuthering height', as Churchill later called him), who valiantly defended the Corporation's editorial independence. *The Times* managed to publish an edition on 5 May – a single stylographed page with two columns of typewritten news. It cost tuppence, and was snapped up wherever it went on sale.

OVER A HOT STOVE
Ladies Gisborough, Malcolm and Mountbatten in the field kitchens in Hyde Park. Lady Mountbatten (third from left) looks rather overdressed for the job. A few years later, in the hungry 1930s, aristocratic ladies would be making charitable visits to soup kitchens. But for now, they showed their solidarity with the middle and upper classes by doling out lunch to government volunteers. Hyde Park was the centre of the government operation to distribute supplies in London during the strike. It was converted into a kind of army base, with guards on the gates, prefabricated barrack rooms and a motor pool. For the well-to-do ladies helping out, Hyde Park was also conveniently close to home.

The shortage of news inevitably led to some wild speculation and rumours. In the first days of the strike, a story spread that a policeman had been killed when strikers overturned an omnibus. No such thing had happened. In fact, there was very little violent conflict between the factions during the strike, despite the fierce pickets and armoured cars on the streets. If this was a revolution, it was a rather polite, very British kind of revolution – a fact noted with satisfaction by George V, who wrote in his diary that '... our dear old country can be well proud of itself. It shows what wonderful people we are.' Indeed, the King was more even-handed in his attitude to the strikers than many among the upper and middle classes, saying: 'Try living on their wages before you judge them.'

Such violence as did occur was mostly directed against property. Shops were attacked and looted in Glasgow – tellingly, the most frequently stolen items were men's boots. In London, a printer was arrested for manhandling the driver of a van distributing *The British Gazette*, and then trying to slash the van's tyres. In Castleford a schoolmistress named Isabel Brown was charged with sedition after

making a speech in praise of communism. In court she gave her address as 'Moscow, Soviet Russia'. The unlikely poster boy of the government side was Lord Raglan, who was applauded for presenting himself as a humble volunteer at a railway depot and driving a train from Pontypool Road to Monmouth.

On 11 May, the unions brought out the 'second-line workers': engineers, shipbuilders, woodworkers, textile workers, postmen and those in the distributive trades. Three million workers were now on strike, but the action had already failed in its main aims. The country was still functioning, the strikers had failed to gain the sympathy of the population at large – and the government had not budged an inch on the question of the miners. Two days later, TUC leaders offered to call off the strike as a prelude to further negotiations. Despite not receiving any government assurances or guarantees, they called off the strike anyway. The miners held out on their own for seven months until privation and hunger drove them back to the pits to cut coal for longer hours and much reduced wages.

STANDING ROOM ONLY
In the absence of the usual buses, these office workers (above) seem to be enjoying the experience of commuting in a steam-powered lorry. The chuffing lorry looks a slightly more prestigious place to be than in the cattle-cart it is towing behind. These three self-satisfied men (right), standing at the front of a steam engine at Waterloo Station, seem quite content to swap their usual work to become volunteer train drivers. The 'BBB' daubed on the engine's nose refers to their surnames – Bellairs, Barton and Bruce.

continued on page 155

HERE COMES THE FLOOD

A lorry ferries a cargo of passengers across the floodwaters of the River Lea in East London in January 1928, while a crowd of hopefuls await their turn for a ride. The four young boys have shown more individual enterprise by building their own raft.

Just after New Year in 1928, England was hit by floods that the government later described as 'without precedent in the previous 700 years'. The inundation was caused by the sudden thaw of a great volume of snow, accompanied by heavy rain and high tides, causing the Thames and lesser London rivers to burst their banks. When the Thames embankment gave way near Lambeth Bridge, a sudden, freezing torrent gushed through riverside streets, flooding lower floors. Fourteen Londoners drowned at Westminster, Putney and Hammersmith, most of them domestic servants living in basements that flooded so quickly there was no chance of escape. At the riverside Tate Gallery floodwaters damaged artworks stored in the basement and the Houses of Parliament also sustained water damage. Roads were closed for days throughout the Thames Valley, and as far away as Norwich and Nottingham. When the waters eventually receded the government promised to take measures to prevent a similar catastrophe occurring in the capital in the future.

The following year, 1929, did not see literal floods, but in the autumn of that year the fiscal dams gave way in the USA, unleashing an economic tidal wave that crashed on Britain and the rest of the world. The Wall Street Crash marked the true end of the 1920s, although officially the decade had a few weeks more to run. The grim 1930s had begun.

WRITERS AND ARTISTS

The 1920s were a decade of liberating experiments in the arts. The year 1922 saw two literary landmarks: the publication, in Paris, of James Joyce's *Ulysses* and T S Eliot's modernist poem, *The Waste Land*. The following year Aldous Huxley (left) burst on the scene with *Antic Hay*, a glittering satire expressing the disillusion of the post-war decade. The book, like much of 1920s output, was described as 'decadent', a term of abuse or praise, depending on your point of view.

BLAZING A TRAIL
The novelist and poet James Joyce, seen here (below right) with Sylvia Beach, an American who founded the 'Shakespeare and Company' bookshop in Paris and gave *Ulysses* its first publication. Joyce is credited with several innovations in the novel, notably with the 'stream of consciousness' voice, but around the same time Virginia Woolf (above) also made interior monologue an indispensable novelistic tool. Her insistence that a woman writer needs 'a room of her own' to create fiction mirrors the advancing emancipation of women in the 1920s. Woolf was the lover of another eminent woman writer, Vita Sackville-West (below), whose life and personality inspired Woolf's novel *Orlando*. Lesbianism was central to the life and work of Marguerite Radclyffe Hall (left, standing), shown here with her lover Una Troubridge. Her novel, *The Well of Loneliness*, was a plea for sexual tolerance; it was banned on grounds of obscenity.

HUMAN FORMS

Visual artists of the Twenties were at least as experimental as the writers, and attracted similar controversies. Augustus John (top left) had been a war artist, producing fine images of ordinary soldiers. After the war he began to concentrate on portraiture, and was criticised for unflattering – his supporters would say 'honest' – portrayals of his subjects. Eric Gill (bottom left) was attacked for the apparent sexual overtones of his work. His personal sex life might be considered shocking by the standards of almost any decade, but this is totally sublimated in his sculptures, which are sublimely beautiful. Here he is working on the figures of Prospero and Ariel, which adorn the entrance to Broadcasting House, the BBC's headquarters in London.

American-born Jacob Epstein (far right) settled permanently in Britain in 1905 and became one of the century's leading portrait sculptors. Many of his works – such as 'Day and Night', two nude modernist figures on a new office building unveiled in London in 1929 – drew angry accusations of obscenity from both the public and the press. Some of his works were even defaced and vandalised. Epstein was briefly associated with Vorticism, a futurist British art movement co-founded by Percy Wyndham Lewis (above). During the 1920s Lewis put more of his energies into writing than art.

THE DECADE'S END

The last years of the decade were altogether more sombre than the first. It is tempting to speculate that there was a general premonition of darker economic clouds gathering overseas. In the United States of America, frenzied stock market activity fuelled an economic boom through the 1920s that came to a sudden and catastrophic end in October 1929. Share prices collapsed, banks failed and the US economy imploded. One by one, all the trading nations of the world were sucked into the vortex of economic depression. But even before that cataclysm impacted on this side of the Atlantic, something had changed in the zeitgeist. Having fun, so fashionable in Britain at the start of the decade, went out of vogue. Noël Coward managed, as usual, to express the altered mood in a few words:

> 'I'm getting tired of jazz tunes,
> Monotonous,
> They've gotten us
> Crazy now.
> Though they're amusing as tunes
> Music has gone somehow ...'

Britain's long, heady party had petered out and a kind of nationwide hangover had set in. Politically, there was a retreat from confrontation and a general shuffling towards the centre ground. The Labour Party, chastened by the failed militancy of its own left-wingers, settled down to the task of making itself a respectable, electable alternative to the Tories.

Conservative achievements

The ruling Conservatives, for their part, realised in the wake of the General Strike that a little social conscience was in order. The major achievements of Stanley Baldwin's second term were the Pensions Act of 1928, put forward by Neville

ENJOYING THE BREEZE
Late in the decade, young women like these, trying to light their cigarettes on the windy beach at Aldeburgh in Suffolk, suddenly found that they were allowed to vote as well as smoke. In 1927, the Conservative government declared that the voting age for women was to be lowered to 21, the same as for men. The move took everyone by surprise, partly because the historic change was announced in a rather offhand way, but also because it was assumed that younger voters would naturally favour any party but the Tories. But it did away with the absurd anomaly whereby a woman could become an MP in her twenties, but not vote for one.

Chamberlain, and the Local Government Act of 1929. This made the regional local authorities responsible for the destitute, and so put an end to the archaic and hated Poor Laws.

A third accomplishment of Baldwin's second spell in office was the sudden and unexpected lowering of the voting age for women from 30 to 21 – a change that finally gave women equal franchise status with men. There was, predictably, a flurry of outrage and scare-mongering when the announcement was first made. The *Daily Mirror* warned of 'flapper vote folly', though flappers were already somewhat passé by this time. Others spoke even more condescendingly, not to say anachronistically, of 'petticoat government': no woman in her twenties had worn petticoats for years.

Passing of the old guard

Emmeline Pankhurst, the commanding field marshall of female suffrage, lived just long enough to see the new voting bill pass into law. When she died, in June 1928, her obituary in *The Times* was generous and respectful: 'Whatever views may be held as to the righteousness of the cause to which she gave her life, there can be no doubt about the remarkable strength and nobility of her character … Whatever peril and suffering she called upon her followers to endure, up to the extreme indignity of forcible feeding, she herself was ready to face, and did face, with unfailing courage.'

In 1926 Germany was admitted to the League of Nations, and the Great War seemed done with at last. Paradoxically, the sense of closure gave rise to new assessments of the conflict. Wilfred Owen's pain-filled poetry became more widely known, and his anguished indictment of the 'old lie', that it is 'sweet and proper to die for one's country', slowly became the orthodox view.

Richard Aldington's anti-war and anti-bourgeois novel *Death of a Hero* expressed all the bitterness and anger of a squandered, war-scarred generation. It was published in 1929, the same year that the English translation of *All Quiet on the Western Front* appeared. The tone of Erich Maria Remarque's book – an account of a German platoon's experience at the front – was much gentler than Aldington's book, but the message was no less forceful for that. To British readers it said that war was just as squalid and gruesome whichever side you were on, that the Hun, the former foe, were merely men lost in a muddy hell, just like their British enemy.

Looking to the future

But by the end of the decade there was an entire generation of adults who had not taken part in the war, and therefore knew very little about the reality of it. If there was a gulf in British society in the late Twenties, it was not so much between rich and poor, or north and south, as between those who had suffered the blood and mire of Flanders, and those who had not.

For better or worse, the uncertain future belonged to those who had not – a point made rather lyrically by Winston Churchill in *The World Crisis*, his account of events during the years from 1911 to 1928. Always a prolific and talented writer, Churchill published his five-volume work between 1923 and 1931. 'Merciful oblivion draws its veil', he wrote. 'The crippled limp away; the mourners fall back into the sad twilight of memory. New youth is here to claim its rights, and the perennial stream flows forward, as if the tale were all a dream.'

AUF WIEDESEHEN, PET
Late in 1929 the last of the British troops left the occupied German Rhineland, and the last visible vestige of the Great War departed with them. The men in this picture are a new generation of Tommy: both they and the German girls waving them off are too young to have taken part in the war between their countries. Reconciliation was in the air, and to many it seemed hopeful that Britain and Germany would henceforth be friends to each other. But just three years later a new leader – Adolf Hitler – came to power in Germany, and the old international enmities stirred again. Lasting peace would only be found after a new and even more terrible war.

INDEX

PICTURE ACKNOWLEDGEMENTS

Abbreviations: t = top; m = middle; b = bottom; r = right; c = centre; l = left

All images in this book are courtesy of Getty Images, including the following which have additional attributions:
35t, 69: Sean Sexton
43b, 47t, 92t, 95b, 131b, 153: Popperfoto
47b, 88t: Time & Life Pictures
116-117, 119b: John Kobal Foundation
119m: Redferns
151r: Agence France Presse

LOOKING BACK AT BRITAIN
DECADENCE AND CHANGE – 1920s
is published by The Reader's Digest Association Ltd,
London, in association with Getty Images and
Endeavour London Ltd.

Copyright © 2009 The Reader's Digest Association Ltd

The Reader's Digest Association Ltd
11 Westferry Circus
Canary Wharf
London E14 4HE
www.readersdigest.co.uk

Endeavour London Ltd
21–31 Woodfield Road
London W9 2BA
info@endeavourlondon.com

Written by
Jonathan Bastable

For Endeavour
Publisher: Charles Merullo
Designer: Tea Aganovic
Picture editors: Jennifer Jeffrey, Franziska Payer Crockett
Production: Mary Osborne

For Reader's Digest
Project editor: Christine Noble
Art editor: Conorde Clarke
Indexer: Marie Lorimer
Proofreader: Ron Pankhurst
Pre-press account manager: Dean Russell
Product production manager: Claudette Bramble
Production controller: Sandra Fuller

Reader's Digest General Books
Editorial director: Julian Browne
Art director: Anne-Marie Bulat

Colour origination by Chroma Graphics Ltd, Singapore
Printed and bound in China

We are committed both to the quality of our
products and the service we provide to our customers.
We value your comments, so please do contact us on
08705 113366 or via our website at
www.readersdigest.co.uk

If you have any comments or suggestions about
the content of our books, email us at
gbeditorial@readersdigest.co.uk

CONCEPT CODE: UK 0154/L/S
BOOK CODE: 638-010 UP0000-1
ISBN: 978 0 276 44398 5
ORACLE CODE: 356900010H.00.24